Embellishing
with
Felted Wool

16 Projects with Appliqué, Beads, Buttons & Embroidery

MARY STORI

C&T PUBLISHING

Text and Artwork copyright © 2008 by Mary Stori

Artwork copyright © 2008 by C&T Publishing, Inc.

Publisher: Amy Marson

Editorial Director: Gailen Runge

Acquisitions Editor: Jan Grigsby

Editor: Lynn Koolish

Technical Editors: Helen Frost and Ellen Pahl

Copyeditor/Proofreader: Wordfirm Inc.

Design Director/Cover & Book Designer: Christina D. Jarumay

Illustrators: John Heisch and Richard Sheppard

Production Coordinator: Zinnia Heinzmann

Photography by C&T Publishing, Inc., unless otherwise noted

Published by C&T Publishing, Inc., P.O. Box 1456, Lafayette, CA 94549

Library of Congress Cataloging-in-Publication Data

Stori, Mary.

 Embellishing with felted wool : 16 projects with appliqué, beads,

buttons & embroidery / Mary Stori.

   p. cm.

 ISBN-13: 978-1-57120-443-1 (paper trade : alk. paper)

 ISBN-10: 1-57120-443-1 (paper trade : alk. paper)

 1. Beadwork. 2. Quilting. I. Title.

 TT860.S775 2008

 745.594'2--dc22

                    2007017739

Printed in China

10 9 8 7 6 5 4 3 2 1

DEDICATION

In the 1800s, innovative women transformed scraps from wool clothing into clever designs that became known as Penny Rugs. This book is dedicated to their ingenuity and needle skills.

ACKNOWLEDGMENTS

The job of editor is so vital to an author, and I'm indebted to the best of the best, Lynn Koolish, for her expertise and patience. Congratulations to the hard working staff at C&T Publishing for their continued dedication to quilters everywhere.

My thanks are also extended to Bernina of America, National Nonwovens, and Moda Fabrics for their generosity.

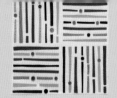

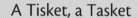

CONTENTS

Introduction

I love the process of beading on fabric, so I'm always looking for new and faster ways to start that process. That might explain my attraction to felted wool. Of course, part of its appeal is that it is soft and cozy, but I especially like working with felted wool because it's not necessary to turn under the edges for appliqué. This time-saver accelerates the construction process and gets me to my favorite part of the project, the beadwork. In addition, because the edges won't fray, my fast-to-do, unique edging techniques can be used instead of traditional quilt bindings. Best of all, this fabric is a perfect backdrop for beads and buttons that contribute to the design by adding color, texture, and sparkle. These decorative elements can also be used to attach wool motifs to the design surface, thereby serving a dual purpose.

My fondness for Penny Rugs, the popular mid-nineteenth century folk art style of wool appliqué, led me to update that classic with a new collage style. The name Penny Rug was earned from the coins used as templates for the circles of graduated sizes that were often featured, along with simple flowers, fruits, and animals. Sometimes pennies where even stitched beneath an appliqué motif to make the piece lie flat. Traditionally, the rugs were finished with tongues, or rounded flaps that created scalloped edges. These hand blanket-stitched and embroidered rugs were actually used on tabletops.

What's old is new again, and today wonderful results can be achieved with 100% wool felt, readily available felted wool blends, or a combination. I've created collage designs suitable for small wallhangings, table toppers, pillows, small purses, scissors sheaths, and business card cases, featuring traditional, folk art, and contemporary styles. It's a coin toss whether you'll be able to stop at one!

My goal is to share projects featuring my innovative, foolproof construction and edging methods. Once you're familiar with the basics, you can easily incorporate them into your own designs, no matter what your skill level or beading experience. Choose the portability and leisure of handwork, or take a faster approach by machine stitching. It's your choice.

I know you'll enjoy working with the warmth of wool, the appeal of embroidery, the charm of buttons, and the pizzazz of beads.

Mary Stori

Basic Supplies and Equipment

Wool Felt

What is felt? In simple terms, it's wool fibers that have matted and tangled together. This happens when wool is subjected to moisture, heat, and pressure. The results are a loftier, fuller fabric with edges that don't need to be turned under when appliquéing because they don't fray. For consistently good results, be sure to work only with felted wool or a felted wool blend, rather than acrylic or polyester craft felt.

100% WOOL

Check your local quilt shop or fabric store for wool prints and solids that are packaged in convenient sampler bundles by fabric companies such as Moda. Mottled, hand-dyed wool may also be available in stores, or look for this style on specialty Internet sites. A good resource when shopping for yardage is chain fabric stores. Look for wool that has a tight weave to prevent the edges from unraveling. Most 100% wool has not been felted (including many of the hand-dyes) and may not be dense enough to act as the main background fabric as purchased. But it's a snap to felt most of these products yourself (see at right). However, the fine weave of suiting fabrics (used for jackets, pants, or skirts) do not tend to felt well.

Look for wool in both solid and woven patterns.

FELTING 100% WOOL

Don't overlook recycling your old blankets, sweaters, and other clothing items. All wool will shrink during the felting process, both in length and width. It can shrink as much as 8″–12″ per yard for 100% wool. The exact amount will vary, depending on the type of wool used.

Here's how to felt woven or knit 100% wool:

1. Fill the washing machine with hot water and about 1 tablespoon of detergent. The addition of ¼ to ½ cup of baking soda during the wash cycles can sometimes help loosen the fibers so they will felt better.

2. Add the wool, and run through a full cycle, making sure the detergent is rinsed out completely. As these slippery wool fibers move against each other with agitation, they get hopelessly tangled together. When dried, they'll become a very sturdy material.

3. Tumble dry at the hottest setting.

4. Press with steam to remove wrinkles, if necessary, or remove when slightly damp. Lay out the felt on towels to dry.

5. Repeat Steps 1–4 if the wool didn't felt well enough during the first cycle.

COMMERCIALLY FELTED WOOL BLENDS

Wool blends that have already been felted are readily available in a wide range of colors for a moderate price. The fabric's appearance may be somewhat flatter than 100% wool felt. To create a more substantial appearance and to add strength, process (felt) it again. Wool blends may lose 3″–5″ inches in length per yard and 2″–4″ across a 36″ width. **Always** process colors separately (or process similar colors together). It's common for the dye to release into the water, altering the colors, especially if working with lights and darks in the same batch.

National Nonwovens (see Resources, page 55) manufactures WoolFelt, a wool/rayon blend, which I use often. Their 20% wool/80% rayon felt is slightly more economical than their 35% wool/65% rayon felt. A 50% wool/50% rayon felt is also available and is so durable that taxidermists use it. National Nonwovens has recently duplicated their felted blends in a limited number of colors to resemble hand-dyed woven wool.

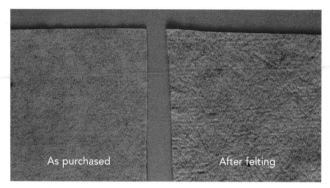

As purchased   After felting

Notice appearance of wool blend fabric as purchased and after further felting.

REFELTING WOOL BLENDS
National Nonwovens Method

(Reprinted by permission.)

Use only WoolFelt styles WCF001 (20/80 blend) and TOY002 (35/65 blend) with this method. To avoid future shrinkage, dry cleaning your finished project is recommended. WoolFelt should be washed only once to create the fleecelike effect.

1. Use cold water to completely wet the WoolFelt in a sink or basin. Do not rub or agitate. Wet each color separately (some dye may be released into the water; this is normal).

2. Squeeze the WoolFelt by hand to remove as much water as possible. Avoid wringing, as it may stretch the material.

3. Dry the WoolFelt in a standard tumble clothes dryer on regular setting until it is nearly dry (approximately 35 minutes). Do not over dry. Dry light colors separately from darker colors. Colors may change slightly during drying process. If excess dye remains in the dryer, take out the WoolFelt, place an old wet towel in the dryer, and finish the dryer cycle to remove any remaining dye.

4. Lay the WoolFelt flat to dry completely, smoothing fabric gently by hand. Large wrinkles may be removed by using a light steam iron held just above the surface of the fabric. If you don't like the effect, you can return felt to its original, flatter form by pressing with a steam iron.

Mary's Refelting Method

1. Fill the washing machine with enough very warm or hot water to cover the fabric.

2. Add the fabric, and soak for about 15 minutes, agitating on gentle about 15 seconds every 5 minutes. Do **not** over agitate, or you'll end up with Santa Claus's beard!

3. Rinse and spin.

4. Tumble dry at the hottest setting until the fabric is dry or damp dry. To avoid setting wrinkles, take out the fabric while it's slightly damp, and lay it out on towels to dry. Or, if the wool has dried completely, press using a steam iron and a pressing cloth. This method usually results in a slightly fuzzier nap.

Felting Hints

- Wash colors separately, as many will bleed.

- Place a lint trap on the washer's discharge hose if it's accessible, and drain the water into a sink. Clean the lint trap after every load.

- Clean the dryer's lint trap often.

- Check to be sure no dye residue remains in the washer or dryer at the conclusion of the felting process.

- Press the felted wool using a pressing cloth or a piece of muslin (with or without steam). Use an up-and-down motion to avoid stretching.

- Hover over the fabric with the iron on a high steam setting to remove minor wrinkles.

- Check carefully for fade lines that often show up where the wool had been folded. They may become more apparent after felting. Mark them with a safety pin to remind yourself to avoid this section or to use the reverse side.

Buttons

Buttons with two or four holes can easily be incorporated into wool collage designs. Shank buttons, however, are not suitable. I use many types and sizes of buttons, from ordinary recycled clothing buttons to antique or decorative styles that feature carving or interesting shapes. The eye-catching finishes of pearl or shell buttons are some of my favorites. Clean up garage sale or flea market finds by washing the buttons gently in soapy water; then rinse and pat dry. Consider infusing additional color into projects by using hand-dyed wood, bone, or plastic buttons in a variety of colors.

Buttons: new, antique, recycled, and flea market finds

Beads

Choose beads to complement your project. There is no absolute right or wrong style, color, or finish. Some of my favorite seed beads are size #11 and the larger size #6. Size #3 bugle beads (about ¼″ in length) can also be easily incorporated. Avoid large heavy beads as decorative elements because of their physical and visual weight, especially if the project is a wallhanging. I always use seed beads to attach buttons for a finished look (see page 16).

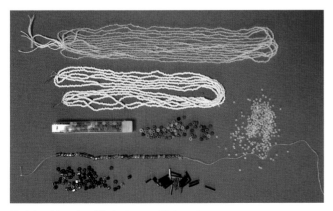

Variety of beads adds texture and interest.

Needles

You'll need several types of needles for hand sewing.

- For beading, use a quilting between or an appliqué needle, also called a sharps or straw needle. I prefer a Jean S. Lyle Quilting Between, size #10, because the eye easily passes through all but the smallest seed beads (see Resources, page 55).

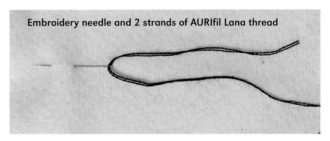

Embroidery needle and 2 strands of AURIfil Lana thread

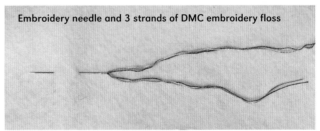

Embroidery needle and 3 strands of DMC embroidery floss

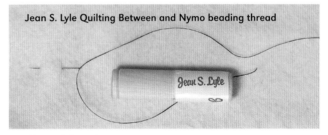

Jean S. Lyle Quilting Between and Nymo beading thread

Needles and threads

- For hand embroidery, you'll need to select a hand-embroidery needle with an eye large enough to accommodate your choice of embroidery thread.

Thread

BEADING THREAD

For beading, I use Nymo beading thread, size D. The thread will be less visible if you match the color to the bead or button, or you can work with a neutral gray or tan color.

EMBROIDERY FLOSS

For hand blanket-stitching around the edges of the wool, 100% cotton DMC six-strand embroidery floss works well. The number of strands used will be determined by the desired effect you wish to achieve; for more visibility, increase the number of strands.

WOOL-BLEND EMBROIDERY THREAD

For hand or machine stitching, wool-blend embroidery thread blends nicely with felted wool. Either of the following two brands will offer good results. (See Resources on page 55.)

- AURIfil Lana thread 50% acrylic/50% wool, 12-weight (For machine work, use a size 16 topstitch needle.)

- DMC Medicis 100% wool (A single strand will result in delicate stitches; use several strands for a bolder outline.)

ALL-PURPOSE SEWING THREAD

An all-purpose thread is suitable to baste both the stabilizer and the design motifs to the main background fabric. I like white because it's easy to see. When incorporating machine stitching, let your personal preference of thread brand and style be your guide. Be sure to test its performance on wool scraps before committing to the actual project.

Stabilizer

Use a lightweight tear-away stabilizer with a little drape to it to provide support for embellishments and to prevent stretching or distortion of the wool. The stabilizer is usually not removed, except near the edges where it might be seen peeking out between the layers or when the front and back layers are fused together. Therefore, you'll want to avoid stiff, heavy-weight stabilizers that are intended for machine embroidery unless your project requires extra strength. The following types of products work equally well for both hand and machine sewing.

- Pattern tracing material (most often used for tracing garment patterns), such as HTC Pattern Ease or HTC Red Dot Tracer

- Lightweight tear-away stabilizer (nonwoven), such as Sulky Tear-Easy or Pellon Lightweight Stitch-N-Tear

- Cut-away stabilizer (polymesh), such as OESD Poly Mesh Cut-Away Embroidery Stabilizer or Sulky Cut-Away Soft 'n' Shear

Adhesives

To secure the front and back layers together and to attach design motifs in preparation for hand embroidery or beading, use one or more of the following products.

GLUESTICK

Apply gluestick to the wrong side of a motif to temporarily hold it in place. Use only when the designs will be stitched within a few hours; otherwise, the glue will dry out quickly due to the wool's porous surface.

PAPER-BACKED FUSIBLE WEB

Quickly transfer patterns and design motifs onto the felted wool with fusible web. When cut and fused, the motif's edges are permanently bonded, providing a tidier appearance and hassle-free hand or machine blanket-stitching experience. I've had good results with Wonder-Under. It bonds well without too much stiffness and is easy to sew through.

SPRAY ADHESIVES

I usually avoid spray adhesives because I'm not willing to accept the overspray mess in my workspace. However, when embellishing with a lot of buttons and beads, fusing may not always be practical, and spray basting can be an efficient substitute to hold the layers together.

Marking Tools

Choose a marking tool that draws a fine line and is easily removed. Powdered chalk marking tools, such as Clover's Chaco-Liner and EZ's Chalk Wheel, deposit chalk in fine lines, which are helpful when transferring complex patterns. Good old-fashioned soap slivers are always handy to have on hand. Avoid brands that contain cold cream because they crumble too easily. Wool is too fuzzy to get a good line with a marking pencil.

Marking tools

Place soap slivers in the refrigerator until they are cold, and then use a vegetable peeler to narrow an edge to get a thinner marked line.

To prevent chalk or soap sliver marked lines from disappearing from the front of the project as you work and to add more stability, retrace the lines with hand or machine thread-basting. If the guideline was marked for button placement, simply center the button on the line and stitch. Remove the basting thread after all the buttons are added. (See page 11 for more on basting.)

Create longer-lasting guidelines by thread-basting over chalk or soap marking.

Cutting Equipment

SCISSORS

For clean edges and precision cutting, use small, sharp scissors that cut to the point.

ROTARY CUTTING TOOLS

To avoid excess handling of unstabilized wool, work with the largest cutting mat you have available. Acrylic rulers that are 15″ × 15″ and 6″ × 24″ are usually sufficient. Use your favorite rotary cutter, fitted with a sharp blade. A quick way to get decorative edges is to cut the felted wool using a decorative rotary blade. I've had good luck with the wave and scallop styles.

Templates

PAPER-BACKED FUSIBLE WEB AND FREEZER PAPER

Use either of these products to quickly transfer design elements. Trace the motifs onto paper-backed fusible web or freezer paper, and iron them to the wool using a warm iron. The paper provides the stability so you can cut shapes with clean edges.

MYLAR TEMPLATES

Trace or draw designs, such as baskets, flowers, and leaves, onto Mylar. Then trace around the templates onto your felted wool.

CIRCLE TEMPLATES

Circles can be made by tracing found objects such as coins or bowls or by using templates available at quilt shops, at office supply stores, and from stencil manufacturers. My favorite product is Karen Kay Buckley's Perfect Circles (see Resources, page 55).

Frame

When beading or embroidering large or heavily embellished pieces, I like to secure my projects in a PVC-type frame, such as a Q-Snap Frame (see Resources, page 55). To avoid distortion or damage to previously beaded areas, gently wrap the fabric around the frame, and thread- or pin-baste it in position instead of using the clips. I use both the 11″ × 11″ and 11″ × 17″ sizes.

Secure fabric to PVC frame with safety pins or thread-basting.

Basic Techniques

Design Decisions

Before you begin to cut the fabric, make as many design decisions as possible, including the purpose of the project and its size, shape, motif, theme, color, bead embellishment, and button layout. Don't worry too much about this—you usually can change your mind as you go along.

Look through the designs offered in the following pages. Feel free to combine an embellishment idea from one project with an edging treatment of another. For example, select a motif, such as a button star, and use it to embellish a pillow rather than the small wall quilt.

When choosing the color scheme, make sure the background and foreground fabrics contrast each other. Also audition the colors of all the other appliqué materials, including thread, floss, and beads. In particular, consider the impact of the buttons. White buttons will be more visible on a black background than on a light pastel. Light reflecting off shiny buttons can also enhance their impact in either a positive or a negative manner.

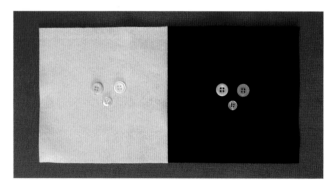

Notice impact of buttons on different background colors.

Preparation

Wool collage projects consist of a minimum of two layers: the front, which is the background for the embellishment, and the back, where the edging treatment is often showcased. Keep in mind that the shape of the front layer often differs from the shape of the back.

Stabilize the Front Piece

Always stabilize the wool piece you will be embellishing with a lightweight tear-away stabilizer (page 8) to help control the distortion that may result from the beading and embroidery. Stabilizer allows you to make nice knots and create uniform stitch tension. The overall shape of the project is documented by marking the stabilizer and basting on those lines. Each project includes instructions on stabilizing the main background. This is an important step; don't skip it.

Transfer Designs

Because the loft of felted wool makes it more difficult to mark clear lines and its density doesn't allow tracing using a light-box, you'll need to use some clever tricks to mark design lines. Choose the method most appropriate to your design and construction method. You might want to begin by marking vertical and horizontal reference lines on the right side of the wool to help keep your collage design properly placed. (*Note:* Test your marking tool on a scrap of felted wool to make sure the lines are removable.)

Mark front of stabilized felt with reference lines to aid in placing motifs. (Basting is demonstrated with pink thread.)

STABILIZER TECHNIQUE

Trace symmetrical designs directly onto the stabilizer, within the boundaries of the marked finished shape of the project. Secure the stabilizer to the wool by thread-basting along all the marked lines to transfer the shape of the project and the placement of the designs to the right side of the wool.

Mark stabilizer and place on wrong side of felt.

Design is visible on top of wool after design is thread-basted along marked lines.

When working with asymmetrical images, trace the design using a black permanent pen. The ink flow of most brands will be visible on both sides of the stabilizer. Simply flip the stabilizer over when positioning it onto the wrong side of the wool to thread-baste the mirror image of your design.

FREEZER-PAPER TECHNIQUE

To transfer a shape such as a basket or heart, trace the shape onto the dull side of freezer paper, and cut out along the marked line. Position the freezer-paper template (shiny side down) onto the right side of the stabilized felted wool. Press with a warm dry iron using a pressing cloth to secure the template to the felted wool. Trace around the outside edge of the template using a soap sliver or a powdered chalk marking tool. Remove the freezer-paper template.

Trace around freezer-paper template.

MARKING-TOOL TECHNIQUE

Intricate, delicate, or single-line patterns can be transferred to the wool background using a metal wheel powdered chalk tool. Begin by tracing the design onto paper, such as blank newsprint, tissue paper, or freezer paper. Cut out the motif with about a $\frac{1}{2}''$ margin. Position the marked paper onto the right side of the stabilized wool, where you want the design to be, and secure the edges of the paper with tape strips or a warm iron if you are using freezer paper. Use a bit of pressure as you run the chalk marking tool over the design lines, perforating the paper as you go to create a marked line on the wool.

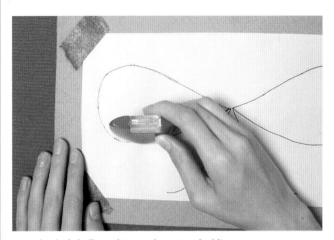

Run wheel of chalk marking tool over marked lines.

Wheel perforates paper to transfer designs.

Mark and Cut Out the Wool Motifs

You'll get the cleanest and most accurately cut edges by cutting through marked paper templates with sharp scissors or a rotary cutter. Use any of the methods described below that best suit your project. (*Note:* You may use more than one method in a project.)

FREEZER-PAPER METHOD

The Freezer-Paper Method is recommended for creating dimensional wool motifs. Trace the motif onto the dull side of freezer paper, and cut it out, leaving at least a ⅛" margin. This is your template. If there are multiple designs, allow a scant ¼" between each motif. Position the freezer-paper templates (shiny side down) onto a piece of felted wool. Press with a warm dry iron using a pressing cloth. Let the wool and freezer paper cool before handling. Cut the shape out through the paper, following the marked line.

Remove the freezer-paper template. Arrange the motif as desired, and temporarily secure it by tacking it in place by thread-basting, pinning with straight pins, or using a dab of gluestick. Choose a beading technique that allows you to attach the motif with beads, leaving the edges free.

Cut freezer-paper templates along marked line; remove freezer paper before attaching motif to project.

When working with freezer-paper templates, rough cut about ⅛"–¼" outside the drawn lines, rather than on them. The felt shapes will have a cleaner edge if you cut through the paper.

PAPER-BACKED FUSIBLE WEB METHOD

When the appliqué process calls for blanket-stitching, use the Paper-Backed Fusible Web Method to attach felt motifs to another piece of wool. The fusible web keeps the edges cleaner, making the embroidery process easier. This approach is handy to use even if you choose not to finish the edges with stitching. Instead, bead embellish the fused motifs just for decorative purposes.

Trace the motif onto the paper side of paper-backed fusible web. Cut around the marked shape, leaving about a ¼" margin. If there are multiple designs, allow a scant ¼" around each motif. Read the manufacturer's instructions for your selected brand of fusible web. In general, use a warm iron to secure the fusible web (paper side up) to the wool. Let the wool cool before handling. Cut out the motif, through the paper, along the marked lines, and remove the paper backing.

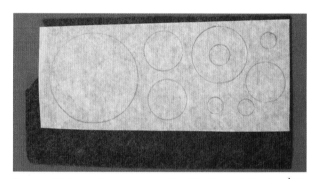

Trace multiple motifs onto paper side of fusible web, leaving ¼" margin between each motif.

After the motifs are arranged to your satisfaction, use a warm iron to fuse them in place permanently. When working with fusibles, it's a good idea to protect your iron and wool by using a Teflon pressing sheet, often sold as an appliqué pressing sheet. Embellish the motifs as desired with embroidery or beads.

Fused motifs are easy to embellish

A Note on Fusing

There are many variables that can affect how fusible adhesive adheres to fabrics. **Always** test the fusible adhesive on your felt scraps. You'll find that because the fiber content and density/thickness of felted materials varies, you may need to adjust your iron temperature and pressing time to achieve a sufficient bond between the layers without damaging any of the materials.

Layout Tips

- Position all the designs within the boundaries of the marked outline of the project edges.

- Use additional basted reference lines to accurately place specific designs.

- Work on a design wall for wallhangings, if possible, or on a flat surface for table toppers.

- Use a digital camera to record placement for later review.

- Physically place the buttons on the marked motif before proceeding. This will ensure that there's an adequate amount of space and buttons. Adjust if necessary.

- To retain the placement, carefully shift or slide the button arrangement onto a firm surface.

Here's another trick I use to retain my button layout: Press strips of tape to pick up rows or sections in your arrangement. It's an easy matter to peel off each button as they are stitched into position.

If the tape is excessively sticky, it may take the finish off pearl or shell buttons. You can reduce the tackiness by adhering and then removing the tape onto a fabric surface a few times before attaching it to the buttons. Or use removable tape.

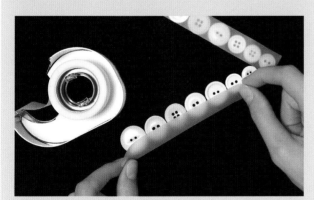

Retain button layout using tape.

Embroidery Techniques

Always test your stitches on a scrap of wool before beginning your project. Experiment with various types, colors, number of strands of threads, and embroidery stitches.

Although there are many variations of embroidery stitches that can be incorporated into the work, I've concentrated on the following three, which I use the most. Feel free to add your favorites.

BLANKET STITCH

This stitch, also known as the Buttonhole Stitch, adapts well for stitching borders and edges, and outlining motifs. It's formed by looping the thread over the needle as the stitch is taken, working horizontally from left to right. When stitching along the edge of a single layer of felted wool, begin in an area that contains two layers of wool, hiding the knot between these layers. Travel as invisibly as possible through the fibers of the single layer to the outside edge. Reverse this process to end the thread.

1. Come up at A, and lay the thread down horizontally to the right. Hold it in place with your thumb.

2. Circle the thread to keep it on the far right side of the needle.

3. Re-enter at B, and come back up at C, with the thread under the point of the needle.

4. Pull through, and repeat the stitches a desired distance apart.

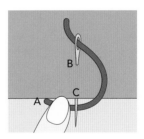

Blanket Stitch

Many sewing machines are now programmed with the Blanket Stitch. Machine stitching can be substituted to secure the edges of fused wool motifs or the fused main wool background section to the wool back. Begin and end with long thread ends, tie off by hand, and bury the knot between the layers.

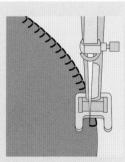

Position fabric to allow horizontal stitches to enter both layers being sewn, while vertical stitches fall along outside edge.

DIAGONAL OVERCAST STITCH

Use this stitch along the outside edges of a project to secure two layers together. Keep the angle of the stitch as uniform as possible, sewing closely together. Pull the stitches snugly, but not too tight, or you'll create a rippled edge. I like how AURIfil thread (see Resources, page 55) fills in and blends with the felted wool for a neatly finished edge.

1. Begin at the upper right corner of the project. Hide the knot between the layers, and exit through the top layer, about ¼" from the corner at A.

2. Wrap the thread diagonally around the outside edge, and come up at B (about ¼" away from A).

3. Wrap the thread diagonally around the edge, and come up at C. Repeat.

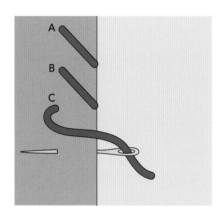

Diagonal Overcast Stitch

STEM STITCH

The Stem Stitch creates crisp lines. The width is determined by the number of strands of floss or thread used. I often mix three shades of a color—for instance, a light, dark, and medium brown—to achieve a tweedy, textured look to the embroidery. The Stem Stitch can be worked as shown. Or it can be worked as an Outline Stitch by holding the thread loop to the right of the needle as you stitch, resulting in a straighter line.

1. Come up at A, holding thread to the left.

2. Go down at B and up at C.

3. Pull through. Go down at D, holding thread to the left.

4. Come up at B (at the end of the previous stitch). Pull through. Repeat.

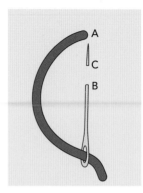 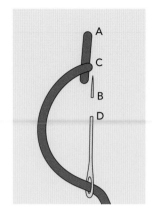

Stem Stitch

Beading Techniques

Here are a few very simple stitches you can use to embellish or bead appliqué your projects. Feel free to explore beading techniques that you may already know, or get acquainted with the many other examples in my previous publications: *Beading Basics, All-in-One Beading Buddy*, and *Mary Stori Teaches You Beading on Fabric* (DVD) (see Resources, page 55).

I recommend using Nymo beading thread, size D, because it's very strong, won't stretch, and is a fairly thin thread. In general, match the thread color to the bead or button, or choose a neutral color such as gray. In some cases, you may need to match the thread color to the fabric, rather than to the bead, to make it blend in.

Whenever possible, hide the knot between the layers of wool or under a button or bead. Travel the thread between layers or between the fibers of a single layer. To hide the stitches and protect the threads, you'll want to do as much stitching as possible on the stabilized front before adding the final back piece. Take care to avoid distorting single layers of fabrics when embellishing with beads.

SINGLE BEAD BACKSTITCH (BEAD APPLIQUÉ)

The all-purpose Single Bead Backstitch can be used to add decorative details or to secure design elements to the project. I call this approach bead appliqué, with the beads contributing to the construction process; you embellish as you appliqué.

1. Pass the knotted, threaded needle from the wrong side to the right side at A. String 1 bead on the thread.

2. Go back down at B, 1 bead width from where the thread came up. The stitch length should be the exact size of the bead.

3. Repeat this process until the desired length is reached.

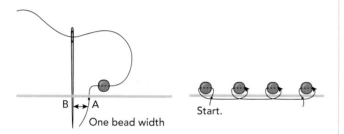

Single Bead Backstitch with seed beads

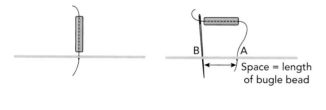

Single Bead Backstitch with bugle beads

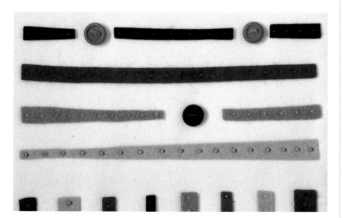

Lines & Circles: Embellish fused wool motifs with Single Bead Backstitch.

BEAD EMBROIDERY STITCH

The Bead Embroidery Stitch is useful when stitching continuous lines of beads to cloth. Its main advantage is that it's less stressful to the fabric—something to consider when working with felted wool that may not be very dense.

1. Work horizontally from right to left to string 5 seed beads,

2. Go down at B (the stitch will equal the length of the beads).

3. Come back up at C (between the 3rd and 4th bead strung).

4. Pass through the last 2 beads, and repeat this process.

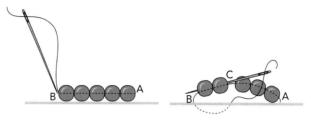

Bead Embroidery Stitch

Feel free to combine different styles of beads to add interest. For example, string 2 seed beads, 1 bugle bead, and 2 seed beads, and then backstitch through the last seed bead; repeat this combination.

Autumn Luster: Attach leaves to main background using Bead Embroidery Stitch.

WASHER/NUT

This versatile Washer/Nut combination secures a bead in position by using a smaller bead, which also helps obscure the thread. The method adds welcome texture and dimension to wool projects.

1. Come up at A.

2. String a large bead and a smaller bead that is larger than the hole of the large bead.

3. Pass the needle back through the hole of the large bead at B and through to the wrong side, bypassing the smaller bead.

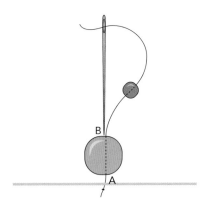

Washer/Nut Technique

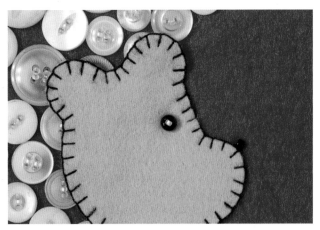

Half Moon Dreams: Use Washer/Nut Technique to create teddy bear's eye.

BEADED BUTTONS

To attach buttons, begin by centering a button on a marked design line and sewing it to the background using one strand of Nymo thread. Placing the holes of the buttons on the line gives a consistent look to rows, even if the buttons are slightly different sizes. Position the next button, and sew in place as if you were sewing a running stitch. Work in rows when filling in a shape, or simply follow the drawn line when outlining a shape. Make a knot about every 10 buttons to keep thread tension taut. Repeat until all the buttons have been positioned satisfactorily on the design. Be very careful not to distort the fabric by pulling the holding thread too tight or by placing the buttons too close to one another.

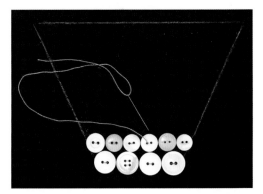

Secure buttons along design line with strand of beading thread (demonstrated with pink thread).

Cover the holding thread by embellishing with beads:

1. Begin with new thread, and come up at A.

2. String enough beads to span the distance to B. Then pass through the hole and fabric. (For buttons with large holes, use enough extra beads to fill them.)

3. Come up at the next button in line and repeat.

4. Make a knot every 6–8 buttons to maintain proper thread tension.

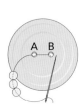

Embellish button with beads.

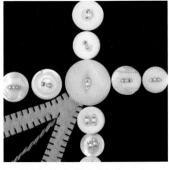

Penny Iris: Embellish 2-hole and 4-hole buttons with beads.

BEAD CLUSTER

Clusters of beads create texture and can add color. Consider using them to attach one wool motif to another, or use them simply as a decorative touch. Because the length of the stitch is less then the length of the string of beads, the beads cluster up on each other when the stitch is pulled tight.

1. Come up at A.

2. String 7 seed beads.

3. Pass the needle through the fabric, about 1 bead distance from where the first bead sits on the fabric.

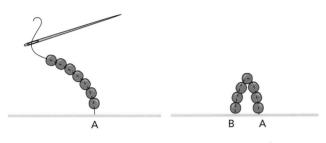

Bead Cluster

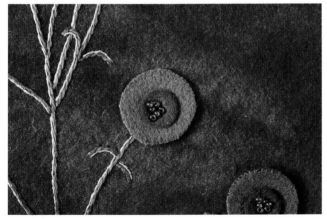

Prairie Flower: **Attach flower heads with Bead Clusters.**

Vary the appearance of Bead Clusters by using more or less beads in each unit. Use uneven numbers, such as three, five, or seven beads.

Finishing Instructions

Remove the basting stitches and any stabilizer that might be visible around the outer edges when the back is attached. Flatten any bulges with a warm iron. Use a pressing cloth when working on the right side to protect the embellished surface and to keep from marking the wool with the iron's sole plate. Or, press the piece flat from the wrong side by placing the project, embellished side down, onto a terrycloth-covered pressing surface. Use a warm iron; a hot iron can melt the beading thread or damage the stabilizer. I only use a hot iron to fuse together areas without beading or to achieve crisp creases on folded edging treatments.

Temporarily attach the front piece to the prepared back using pins, basting stitches, or spray adhesive. This step will help keep the layers together as the project is completed with further beading or embroidery.

If the main body of the project is heavy, use fusible web to bond the front to the back. Trim away as much stabilizer as possible from the back side, removing all the basting lines. Mark a piece of paper-backed fusible web with the desired finished size, and position it with the web side facing the back of the embellished front piece. Follow the manufacturer's directions to fuse the web. After it has cooled, cut through the paper, following the marked line. Remove the paper, and position this piece onto the prepared back piece. Fuse these layers together.

EDGING TREATMENTS

There are many ways to finish the edges of felted wool collage designs (this is part of the fun). Explore the options offered in the projects, and feel free to exchange one edging method for another as desired. The following is a list of general suggestions that will help you incorporate these ideas into your own designs.

- Cut the back the same size and shape as the embellished front piece. Sandwich the layers together, and secure the edges with hand or machine blanket-stitching (see page 21).

- Use the same treatment as described above, further embellishing the project by slipping individual tongues between the front and back layers. This method is reminiscent of traditional Penny Rugs (see pages 52–54).

- Sew the edges of the front and back pieces with right sides together, leaving an opening to turn inside out (see page 20).

- Create a frame for the embellished front by using a different color of wool and cutting the back piece an inch or more larger than the front. Secure the front to the back with beads or stitching. The outside edge of the back can be trimmed to the desired width with a straight cut, or consider using a decorative rotary cutting blade. This frame border can be also be embellished with beads or lightweight buttons (see pages 34, 36, and 39).

- Use the frame treatment as described above, cutting the back several inches larger than the front. With a prepared template, cut the outside edge of the back into large scallops, and finish the edges with hand blanket-stitching (see pages 41, 44, and 47).

Making an Embellished Wool Collage

1. Develop a project and design plan (see Design Decisions, page 10).

2. If necessary, make a template of the overall shape, and stabilize the front piece (see Stabilize the Front Piece, page 10).

3. Transfer the project shape and design motifs to the front piece (see Transfer Designs, pages 10–11).

4. Prepare the wool motifs (see Mark and Cut Out the Wool Motifs, page 12).

5. Arrange the motifs onto the stabilized front piece (see Layout Tips, page 13).

6. Attach the wool designs using the method of your choice, such as fusing, embroidery, or beading (see Paper-Backed Fusible Web Method, page 12; Embroidery Techniques, pages 13–14; Beading Techniques, pages 14–17).

7. Arrange and secure the buttons (see Beaded Buttons, page 16).

8. Bead or hand embroider any further details you might wish to add.

9. Complete the front (see Finishing Instructions, page 17).

10. Finish assembling the project with the desired edging method. For ideas, refer to the various edging options in each project.

Projects

It's a good idea to first look through all the projects and become acquainted with the various approaches. Then, it's your choice whether you want to duplicate some of these design ideas or build your own bead-embellished wool collage.

All the designs begin by securing various collage elements to a single layer of stabilized felted wool. This approach makes the beading and appliqué process easier to accomplish. The stitches are hidden and protected by attaching another layer to the wrong side. The additional piece of wool then becomes the back, a lining, or perhaps just another design element. With so many clever edging options, you might be inspired to try them all.

Due to the weight of beads, buttons, and appliqué motifs—not to mention the size and shape of the work—some designs are better suited for tabletops, pillows, or other accessories, rather than a wallhanging.

Wallhangings require good support across the piece, such as a fabric sleeve sewn to the wrong side.

Sew fabric tube to wrong side of wallhanging as hanging sleeve.

Lines & Circles,
15″ × 15″,
Mary Stori, 2005

Lines & Circles

Turned Edge

THIS CONTEMPORARY DESIGN IS CREATED BY
EVENLY DIVIDING THE MAIN FABRIC SQUARE INTO
FOUR SECTIONS. AN EYE-CATCHING PATTERN
DEVELOPS BY POSITIONING THE BUTTONS AND
BEAD-APPLIQUÉD STRIPS OF WOOL VERTICALLY
AND HORIZONTALLY. THIS DESIGN IS ALSO
PERFECT FOR A PAIR OF PILLOWS.

Materials

Refer to pages 5–9 for basic supplies.

- 1 square 16″ × 16″ of white felted wool for front
- 1 square 15½″ × 15½″ of white felted wool for back
- Scraps of assorted colors of felted wool for appliquéd strips
- 1 square 16″ × 16″ of lightweight tear-away stabilizer
- ½ yard of paper-backed fusible web
- Hand-dyed wooden buttons (approximately 14)
- Variety of seed beads in colors to match wool strips
- Nymo beading thread

Instructions

Refer to pages 10–18 for basic techniques.

PREPARATION

Mark a square 15″ × 15″ centered on the stabilizer, and divide it horizontally and vertically into 4 equal sections. Thread-baste the stabilizer to the white front piece, following the marked lines.

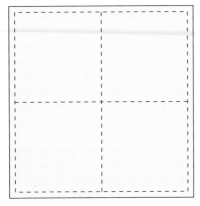

Baste stabilizer to front following marked lines.

COLLAGE AND EMBELLISH

1. Use the Paper-Backed Fusible Web Method (page 12) to prepare the strips, cutting the scraps into strips about ½″ wide. You can make them even or uneven, but be sure to vary the lengths. Remove the paper backing from the strips.

2. Arrange the wool strips and buttons in a pleasing manner on the stabilized front piece. Alternate their placement vertically and horizontally from section to section. (Refer to the project photo.) Keep the strips at least ½″ from the edges of each section and 1″ from the outside basted lines. Set aside the buttons, and fuse the strips to the front piece with a warm iron to prevent movement during the beading process.

Document the layout by taking a digital photograph so you have a record of how to reposition the buttons.

3. Use the Single Bead Backstitch (page 15) to embellish the strips by stitching the seed beads, spaced about a needle's length apart, through all the layers.

4. Use the Beaded Buttons technique (page 16) to attach the buttons.

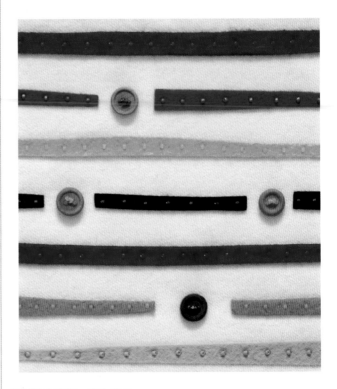

TURNED EDGE

1. Cut the embellished front piece to measure 15½″ × 15½″. Trim the stabilizer from the seam allowance area.

2. Place the front and back pieces right sides together, matching the raw edges. Pin to secure the layers.

3. Machine stitch, using a 2.0 stitch length and a ¼″ seam allowance. Start near the center of one side, and secure with a few backstitches. Stitch around the pieces, stopping 6″ from where you began to leave an opening. End by securing with a few backstitches.

4. Trim the excess bulk from the corners, if necessary, and carefully turn the piece inside out through the opening.

5. Press the edges from the back side to evenly distribute the seams and to even up the edges. Hand stitch to close the opening as invisibly as possible.

Prairie Flower,
8½″ × 11″,
Mary Stori, 2005

Prairie Flower

Straight Even-Edge

THIS SMALL TABLE TOPPER OR WALLHANGING FEATURES HAND-EMBROIDERED STEMS AND BEAD-TOPPED FELT FLOWERS. THE HAND BLANKET-STITCHING ADDS A COZY TOUCH TO THE SOFTNESS OF THE FELTED WOOD.

Materials

Refer to pages 5–9 for basic supplies.

- 1 rectangle 9½″ × 12″ of blue hand-dyed felted wool for front
- 1 rectangle 8½″ × 11″ of blue hand-dyed felted wool for back
- Scraps of putty color and olive green felted wool for circle flowers
- 1 rectangle 9½″ × 12″ of lightweight tear-away stabilizer
- Embroidery thread or floss in tan and olive green
- Variety of seed beads in colors to match or contrast wool scraps
- Nymo beading thread
- Freezer paper

Instructions

Refer to pages 10–18 for basic techniques.

PREPARATION

1. Mark a rectangle 8½″ × 11″ centered on the stabilizer. Thread-baste the stabilizer to the blue front piece, following the marked lines.

2. Use the Marking-Tool Technique (page 11) to transfer the stem motif from Side A of the pullout at the back of the book onto the right side of the stabilized front piece.

COLLAGE AND EMBELLISH

1. Hand embroider along the marked lines, using the Stem Stitch (page 14) and 3 strands of olive green embroidery floss. To provide dimension to the stems, embroider another line of stitching along the edge of the first, using 2 strands of tan floss.

2. Use the Freezer-Paper Method (page 12) to cut 11 putty-colored 1″ circles and 11 olive green ⅝″ circles from the wool scraps.

3. Stack 1 large and 1 small circle to represent flower heads at the end of each stem. Secure by bead-appliquéing in position, using the Bead Cluster technique (page 17).

STRAIGHT EVEN-EDGE/BLANKET STITCH EMBROIDERY

1. Cut the embellished front piece to measure 8½″ × 11″. Trim away the stabilizer from the outside edges.

2. Layer the embellished front and the back together, temporarily securing with thread-basting or spray adhesive.

3. Finish the edges with hand or machine blanket-stitching (page 13). Try to position the corner stitches in a consistent manner.

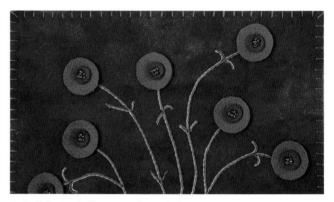

Embellish simple flowers with Bead Clusters.

Scissors Sheath,
3″ × 6½″,
Mary Stori, 2006

Scissors Sheath

Shaped Edge

PROTECT YOUR SCISSORS WITH THIS FAST-TO-MAKE CARRYING CASE. THIS SHEATH FITS SCISSORS MEASURING ABOUT 5″ IN LENGTH, BUT YOU CAN ADJUST IT AS NEEDED FOR OTHER SIZES. THIS IS A GREAT GIFT FOR YOUR QUILTING AND CRAFTING FRIENDS.

Materials

Refer to pages 5–9 for basic supplies.

- 3 rectangles 3½″ × 7″ of purple felted wool for front, back, and lining
- Scraps of yellow, red, and turquoise felted wool for stars
- 1 rectangle 3½″ × 7″ of lightweight tear-away stabilizer
- 3 squares 2″ × 2″ of paper-backed fusible web
- 3 white shell buttons ½″ diameter
- 3 each of size #11 seed beads in yellow, red, and turquoise
- Size #11 yellow seed beads for starburst lines
- AURIfil Lana thread in purple
- Nymo beading thread
- Freezer paper

Instructions

Refer to pages 10–18 for basic techniques.

PREPARATION

1. Use the Freezer-Paper Technique (page 11) to prepare 2 scissors sheath templates, using the patterns on Side A of the pullout at the back of the book. Press each onto a purple piece, and cut out along the marked line. (*Note:* These pieces are the back and the lining for the front.)

2. Using the sheath template again, center and trace it onto the tear-away stabilizer. Thread-baste the stabilizer to the remaining purple piece for the front, following the marked line.

COLLAGE AND EMBELLISH

1. Use the Paper-Backed Fusible Web Method (page 12) to prepare the star motifs, using the pattern on Side A of the pullout at the back of the book.

2. Remove the paper backing from the prepared stars, and position them within the basted outlines of the stabilized front (refer to the project photo). Fuse the stars in place with a warm iron.

3. Center and attach a shell button on each star, using seed beads that match the color of the star (page 16).

4. Use the Single Bead Backstitch (page 15) to stitch yellow seed beads about ⅛″ apart (refer to the project photo for placement).

 tip

Use the tip of a needle or a fingernail to mark a line to follow for beading.

SHAPED EDGE/BLANKET STITCH EMBROIDERY

1. Cut out the sheath, following the marked line on the stabilizer. Take care not to cut any of the beading thread. Trim away the stabilizer from the outside edges. With the aid of the original template, mark the top opening with a straight pin on each side.

2. Position the 2 previously cut sheath pieces beneath the embellished front piece. Thread-baste all 3 layers together below the pins. Baste only the top 2 layers together above the pins.

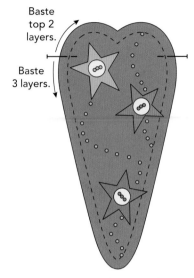

Baste together prepared scissors sheath layers.

3. Use a Blanket Stitch (page 13) and 3 strands of purple thread to stitch the edges together by hand. Work left to right on the front, with the pointed end away from you. Begin at A, hiding the knot in between the top 2 layers at the opening's reference pin. Blanket-stitch only the top 2 layers to B, then stitch through all 3 layers until you reach A. Continuing with the same thread, blanket-stitch the top edge of the back piece. Hide the knot between the layers.

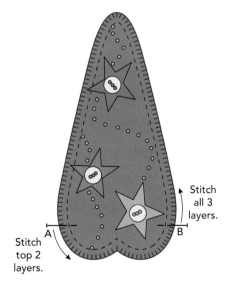

Blanket-stitch edges.

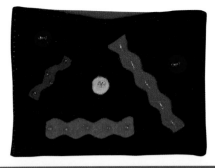

Business Card Holder,
$4\frac{1}{2}'' \times 3\frac{1}{4}''$,
Mary Stori, 2006

Business Card Holder

Straight Edge

SHOW OFF YOUR SKILLS WITH THIS STYLISH BUSINESS CARD HOLDER THAT TAKES ONLY MINUTES TO MAKE.

Materials

Refer to pages 5–9 for basic supplies.

- 2 rectangles $4\frac{1}{2}'' \times 3\frac{1}{4}''$ of black felted wool for front and lining

- 1 rectangle $4\frac{1}{2}'' \times 3\frac{1}{4}''$ of red felted wool for back

- Scraps of assorted colors of felted wool for appliqué motifs

- 1 rectangle $4\frac{1}{2}'' \times 3\frac{1}{4}''$ of lightweight tear-away stabilizer

- Variety of seed beads in colors to match or contrast

- AURIfil Lana thread in black

- Nymo beading thread

- Freezer paper

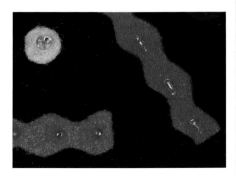

Instructions

Refer to pages 10–18 for basic techniques.

PREPARATION

Baste the lightweight stabilizer to a black piece for the front. (*Note:* Because the wool requires so little handling, you do not need to mark the shape on the stabilizer or allow extra to trim.)

COLLAGE AND EMBELLISH

1. From the scraps, cut several small motifs, such as narrow/short wavy strips and small circles. Arrange in a pleasing manner on the stabilized front piece, securing with a dab of gluestick. Handle carefully to bead-embellish and secure the motifs, using your choice of the beading methods described on pages 14–17.

2. Use the Freezer-Paper Technique (page 11) to prepare 2 templates, using the pattern on Side A of the pullout at the back of the book. (*Note:* Cut out just the rectangular shape following the marked line; do not cut the curved line yet.)

3. Position the freezer-paper templates on the wrong side of the embellished front piece and on the remaining black piece. Secure with a warm iron.

4. Using the marked curved line as a guide, cut through the freezer paper to trim the top edge of each piece. Remove the freezer paper, and trim away the stabilizer from the outside edges of the embellished front piece.

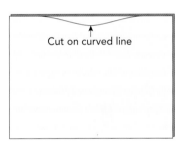

Cut on curved line

Cut top edges of front pieces using freezer-paper templates.

STRAIGHT EDGE/ BLANKET STITCH EMBROIDERY

1. Place the 2 black pieces together, matching the edges. Use pins or spray adhesive to temporarily hold the layers together. Sew around all 4 sides, about $\frac{1}{8}''$ from the raw edges, using a machine straight stitch.

2. Position the stitched piece onto the red back piece, securing with pins or thread-basting as needed. Complete with a decorative Blanket Stitch (page 13), sewing by hand or machine around the sides and bottom edges only.

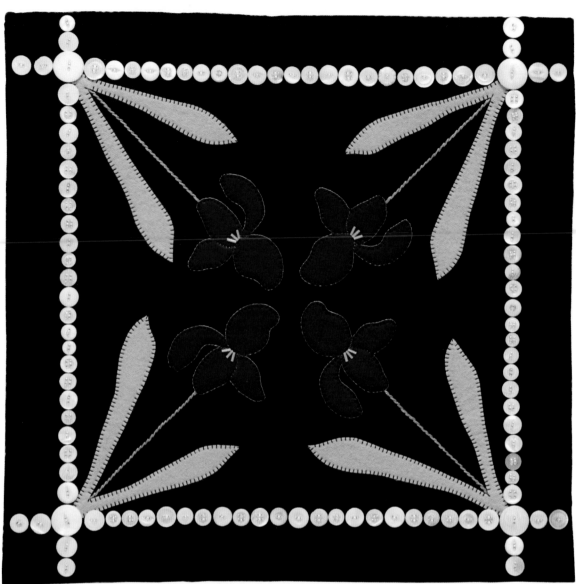

Penny Iris,
16˝ × 16˝,
Mary Stori, 2005

Penny Iris

Straight Even-Edge

FRESH FROM THE GARDEN, THESE IRISES ARE
FENCED IN BY A SWEET BEADED BUTTON
BORDER. MAKE AS A WALLHANGING OR AS
A CHARMING PILLOW.

Materials

Refer to pages 5–9 for basic supplies.

- 2 squares 17˝ × 17˝ of black felted wool for front and back
- 1 square 8˝ × 8˝ of purple felted wool for flowers
- 1 rectangle 10˝ × 12˝ of green felted wool for leaves
- 1 square 17˝ × 17˝ of lightweight tear-away stabilizer
- 1 yard of paper-backed fusible web
- White buttons (approximately 115)
- 12 size #3 yellow bugle beads

- Size #11 white seed beads
- Embroidery floss in green
- AURIfil Lana thread in black
- Nymo beading thread

Instructions

Refer to pages 10–18 for basic techniques.

PREPARATION

1. Mark a square 16″ × 16″ centered on the stabilizer. Mark the button placement lines on the stabilizer by drawing a square 13″ × 13″ centered inside the first square, extending the lines at the corners to the outside edges. Divide the center, horizontally and vertically, into 4 equal sections to mark reference lines for placing the iris motifs.

2. Thread-baste the stabilizer to a black piece for the front, following the marked lines.

COLLAGE AND EMBELLISH

1. Use the Paper-Backed Fusible Web Method (page 12) to prepare the flower and leaf motifs, using the patterns on Side A of the pullout at the back of the book. The patterns are reversed for fusible web appliqué.

2. Arrange the prepared floral motifs, using the project photo as your guide. Fuse in position with a warm iron, and finish the edges, using hand or machine blanket-stitching (page 13).

3. Embellish each flower head with 3 yellow bugle beads, using the Single Bead Backstitch (page 15).

4. Use a small ruler and a marking tool to draw the stems directly onto the wool. Embroider the lines with a Stem Stitch (page 14), using 3 strands of green embroidery floss.

5. Stitch and embellish the buttons to the front on the basted lines, stopping ½″ from the ends to allow for trimming (page 16).

STRAIGHT EVEN-EDGE/OVERCAST EMBROIDERY EDGE

1. Cut the embellished front piece to measure 16″ × 16″, centering the design. Trim away as much of the stabilizer from the wrong side as possible.

2. Cut a square 17″ × 17″ from paper-backed fusible web. Fuse to the remaining black square. Cut into a square 16″ × 16″, and remove the paper.

3. Layer the front and back, with wrong sides together and raw edges matching. Press with a hot iron to secure the layers; be sure to protect the wool and your iron with a pressing sheet.

4. Finish the edges with the Diagonal Overcast Stitch (page 14). Try to position the corner stitches in a consistent manner.

Button Flowerpot,
16″ × 16″,
Mary Stori, 2005

Button Flowerpot

Fold Over/Back-to-Front Edge With Mock Sashing

DELIGHTFULLY OLD-FASHIONED, MIX-AND-MATCH BUTTONS FORM THE FLOWERPOT FOR A LIVELY BUNCH OF BEAD-TOPPED FLOWERS. SCALLOPED SASHING FRAMES THE SCENE.

Materials

Refer to pages 5–9 for basic supplies.

- 1 square 15½″ × 15½″ of brown felted wool for front
- 1 square 18″ × 18″ of green felted wool for back
- 1 square 10″ × 10″ of green felted wool for leaves and stems
- Scraps of red felted wool for flowers
- 4 strips 1″ × 17″ of black felted wool for sashing
- 1 square 15½″ × 15½″ of lightweight tear-away stabilizer
- ½ yard of paper-backed fusible web
- White buttons (approximately 38)

- Size #11 seed beads in black and white
- Size #6 seed beads in black
- Embroidery thread or floss in black
- Nymo beading thread
- Rotary cutter with decorative blade

Instructions

Refer to pages 10–18 for basic techniques.

PREPARATION

Mark a square 14½" × 14½" centered on the stabilizer. Trace the button placement pattern onto the stabilizer, using the pattern on Side A of the pullout at the back of the book. Center the flowerpot outline about 1" above the marked line. Use the Stabilizer Technique (page 11) to thread-baste the stabilizer to the brown front piece, following the marked lines.

COLLAGE AND EMBELLISH

1. Use the Paper-Backed Fusible Web Method (page 12) to prepare the stem and leaf motifs, using the patterns on Side A of the pullout at the back of the book. (*Note:* The stems are cut free-hand.) Refer to the project photo to arrange the motifs, making sure that the top row of the flowerpot buttons will hide the lower ends of the stems.

2. Fuse the motifs onto the stabilized front piece with a warm iron. Finish the edges with hand or machine blanket-stitching (page 13).

3. Cut 26 red felt circles, ranging from ½" to 1" diameter, using the Freezer-Paper Method (page 12).

4. Attach the red circles in a pleasing manner along the stems by stitching size #11 black seed bead units in varying lengths to the centers of each circle, using the Bead Cluster technique (page 17).

5. Arrange and stitch the buttons to fill the shape of the flowerpot outline. When satisfied with the placement, embellish with white seed beads (page 16).

FOLD OVER/BACK-TO-FRONT WITH MOCK SASHING EDGE

1. Cut the embellished front piece to measure 14½" × 14½". Trim away the stabilizer 1" from the outside edges.

2. Center the front piece onto the green back piece. To prevent the front from shifting, temporarily baste the layers together with spray adhesive or thread.

3. Fold the edges of the back to the front, overlapping the front edges by ¼". Overlap or miter at the corners. Measure the width and length of the folded edges, and cut strips of paper-backed fusible web to fit. Remove the paper, and slide the web between the layers. Fuse with a hot iron to secure the back to the front. To strengthen the joined pieces, work from the front and machine stitch the layers together by sewing about ⅛" from the raw edges of the back piece.

Turn back to front, and secure with fusible web.

4. Use a decorative rotary cutting blade to cut 1 lengthwise edge of each black strip to measure ½" wide. (One side will have a straight cut; the other, a decorative edge.) Trim the ends of each strip with a straight cut to measure 16" in length.

5. Center the strips over the raw edges of the green piece, with the wavy edge facing outward. Overlap the strips at the corners. Use straight pins or thread-basting to temporarily hold the strips in place.

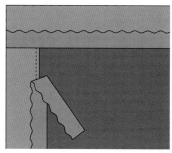

Position strips over edges.

6. Secure the layers together with beads, using the Washer/Nut technique (page 16). Stitch through the layers with stitches about ½" apart. Try to make the stitches on the wrong side as invisible as possible.

Attach mock sashing strip with seed beads.

Autumn Luster, 40˝ × 12˝, Mary Stori, 2004

Autumn Luster

Fold Over/Front-to-Back Edge

BRING THE COLORS OF FALL INTO YOUR HOME
WITH THESE HAND-DYED WOOL LEAVES. THE
LEAVES ARE ATTACHED TO THE TABLE RUNNER
WITH BEADS, ADDING DIMENSION TO THIS
AUTUMNAL SCENE.

Materials

Refer to pages 5–9 for basic supplies.

- 1 rectangle 42˝ × 14˝ of brown felted wool for front
- 1 rectangle 40˝ × 12˝ of 100% cotton print fabric for back
- Small pieces of felted wool in assorted fall colors for leaves
- 1 rectangle 42˝ × 14˝ of lightweight tear-away stabilizer
- ¼ yard of paper-backed fusible web
- Variety of size #11 seed beads and size #3 bugle beads in colors to match leaves
- Nymo beading thread
- Freezer paper

Instructions

Refer to pages 10–18 for basic techniques.

PREPARATION

Mark a rectangle 40″ × 12″ centered on the stabilizer. Thread-baste the stabilizer to the brown front piece, following the marked lines.

COLLAGE AND EMBELLISH

1. Use the Freezer-Paper Method (page 12) to prepare the leaf motifs, using the patterns on Side A of the pullout at the back of the book. Add additional leaf shapes if desired.

2. Arrange the leaves in a pleasing manner, using the project photo as your guide. To retain your design, pin or thread-baste the leaves in position.

3. Use the Bead Embroidery Stitch (page 15) to attach the leaves by stitching lines to represent the leaf veins. Some leaves feature all seed beads, while others have a combination of both seed and bugle beads.

FOLD OVER/FRONT-TO-BACK EDGE

1. Check to see that your original basted rectangle is accurate. If it isn't, mark it with a removable marking tool, and use these new lines as your guide.

2. Baste the piece of cotton fabric to the wrong side of the front piece, lining up the raw edges of the fabric with the basted lines.

3. Due to the weight of the beaded leaves, it's a good idea to machine quilt the layers together. Begin and end the quilting at the basted outline. Avoid dense quilting, which can cause the lines of beads on the leaves to draw up and distort the shape. This is a good time to quilt less, rather than more.

4. Machine stitch along the basted outline. This will help retain the shape.

5. Trim the edges of the embellished front piece with a rotary cutter, leaving a full ½″ of wool outside the stitched line. Trim the stabilizer from the raw edges up to the stitching. Measure the width and length of the turnover allowance. Cut strips of fusible web to fit. Position the strips on the edges of the wool. Fuse to the fabric with a warm iron. Remove the paper backing.

6. Fold the edges to the back, carefully pressing with a hot iron to secure and keep a straight edge.

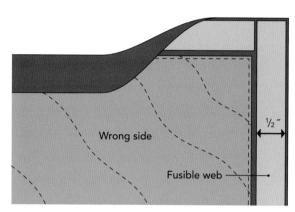

Wrong side

½″

Fusible web

Prepare edges with strips of fusible web.

7. For added strength machine stitch the edges (an edge stitching foot is perfect if you have one). The runner is now complete! If desired—and if you've become smitten with beads—use your favorite beading technique to add them along the edge, as I have done.

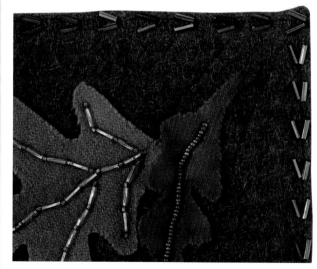

Create finishing touch with beading along outside edge.

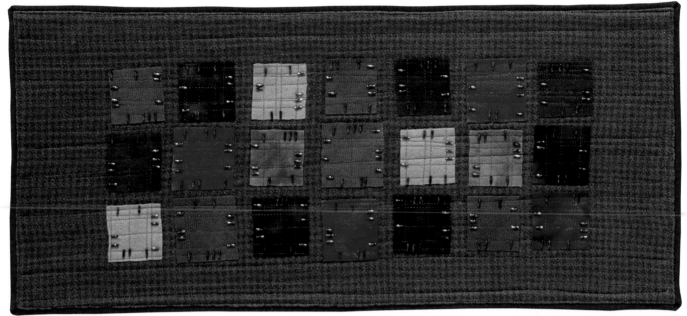

Grid, 25˝ × 11˝, Mary Stori, 2006

Grid

Fold Seam Allowance to Inside Edge

SMALL SQUARES CREATE AN ABSTRACT DESIGN IN
THIS SIMPLE TABLE TOPPER OR WALLHANGING.
THE INTERPLAY OF THE PATTERN AND TEXTURE IS
EMPHASIZED BY MACHINE STITCHING AND
TEXTURED BEADING.

Materials

Refer to pages 5–9 for basic supplies.

- 1 rectangle 26˝ × 12˝ of green plaid felted wool for front

- 1 rectangle 27˝ × 13˝ of red felted wool for back

- Scraps of felted wool prints in coordinating colors for appliquéd squares

- 1 rectangle 26˝ × 12˝ of lightweight tear-away stabilizer

- ⅜ yard of paper-backed fusible web

- Size #3 bugle beads in gunmetal or gray

- Nymo beading thread

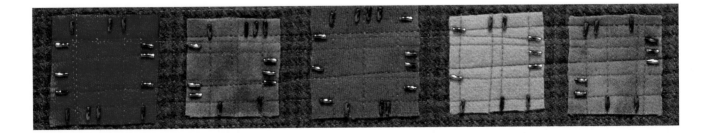

Instructions

Refer to pages 10–18 for basic techniques.

PREPARATION

Mark a rectangle 24½″ × 10½″ centered on the stabilizer. Thread-baste the stabilizer to the green front piece, following the marked lines.

COLLAGE AND EMBELLISH

1. Use the Paper-Backed Fusible Web Method (page 12) to prepare 21 squares 2″ × 2″ from the assorted print scraps. (*Note:* It's not necessary to create perfect 2″ squares; slightly uneven units are fine.) Arrange the units in 3 rows within the basted lines, spacing the squares about ¼″ to ½″ apart, 3¼″ from the short ends, and 1½″ from the long ends.

2. Fuse the motifs onto the stabilized front piece using a warm iron.

3. Machine stitch a grid, horizontally and vertically, spacing the lines a random distance apart and beginning and ending at the edge of the fabric.

4. Embellish the squares with bugle beads in any pattern of your choice, using the Single Bead Backstitch (page 15).

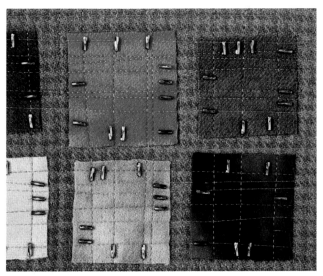

Highlight edges of squares with bugle beads.

FOLD SEAM ALLOWANCE TO INSIDE EDGE

1. Check to see that your original basted rectangle is accurate. If it isn't, mark again, and use these new lines as your guide. With matching thread, machine stitch completely around the rectangle to lock in the grid stitching lines. Cut the front piece, leaving a ¼″ seam allowance beyond the stitched line. Use a hot iron with steam to press the seam allowance to the wrong side, using the stitched line as your guide. Secure with straight pins if necessary.

2. Measure and mark a 25″ × 11″ rectangle on the red wool. Stitch by machine on the lines to mark and stabilize the rectangle shape. Fold on the stitched line, and bring the excess fabric to the front of the back piece. Use a hot iron with steam and press. Miter the corners, and secure with straight pins if necessary.

3. Place the embellished front piece on top of the prepared back piece. The back is slightly larger than the front to provide a frame for the design. Thread-baste or pin the layers together, and machine stitch about ⅛″ from the folded edge of the front to permanently secure the pieces together.

Turn under raw edges of front and back to create finished edge.

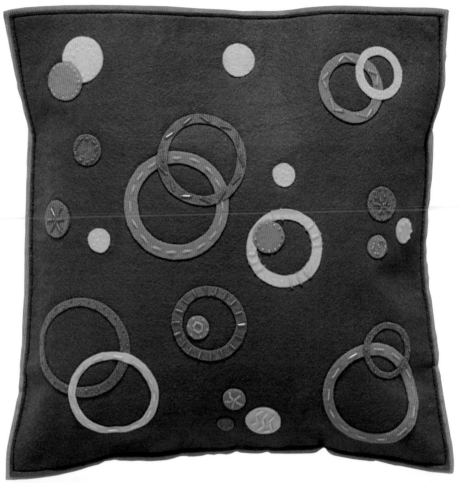

Retro Pillow,
15½″ × 15½″,
Mary Stori, 2006

Retro Pillow

Peek-a-Boo Edge

JAZZ UP YOUR FAVORITE CHAIR OR SOFA WITH THIS RETRO PILLOW, FEATURING BRIGHT RINGS AND CIRCLES. THE PEEK-A-BOO EDGING METHOD PROVIDES A HANDSOME ORANGE FRAME FOR THE PILLOW'S CIRCULAR DESIGNS.

Materials

Refer to pages 5–9 for basic supplies.

- 1 square 16″ × 16″ of green felted wool for pillow front
- 2 rectangles 15″ × 11½″ of green felted wool for pillow back
- Scraps of orange, pink, and yellow felted wool for circle and ring motifs
- 1 square 16″ × 16″ of orange felted wool for Peek-a-Boo edge
- 1 square 16″ × 16″ of lightweight tear-away stabilizer
- ½ yard of paper-backed fusible web
- Variety of size #11 seed beads and size #3 bugle beads in colors to match or contrast wool scraps
- Nymo beading thread
- 14″ × 14″ pillow form

Instructions

Refer to pages 10–18 for basic techniques.

PREPARATION

Mark a square 15″ × 15″ centered on the stabilizer. Thread-baste the stabilizer to the green front piece, following the marked lines.

COLLAGE AND EMBELLISH

1. Use the Paper-Backed Fusible Web Method (page 12) to prepare the ring and circle motifs, using the patterns on Side A of the pullout at the back of the book. I recommend using Karen Kay Buckley's Perfect Circles (see Resources, page 55). Remove the paper backing.

2. Position the motifs as desired on the stabilized front piece, within the basted lines. Fuse the motifs in place using a warm iron.

3. Embellish each circle or ring by stitching beads through all 3 layers (the motif, the front, and the stabilizer), using the Single Bead Backstitch (page 15), or use bead designs of your choice.

PEEK-A-BOO EDGE

1. Cut the embellished front piece to measure 15″ × 15″. Trim away the stabilizer from the outside edges.

2. Center the embellished front piece onto the orange edging square. Pin or baste securely together.

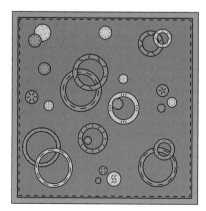

Center and baste embellished front onto edging.

3. Prepare the pillow back by sewing a ½″ hem along a long edge of each green back piece. Place one piece on the orange edging square, with wrong sides together. Use the basted lines as a guide. (*Note:* You are matching the edges of the back piece to the edges of the embellished front piece.) Thread-baste the layers together along the outside edges to make sure the front and back pieces line up properly. Add the second back piece, overlapping the first, and baste along the outside edges.

Position first back piece on wrong side of pillow.

4. Work from the front of the pillow as you machine stitch the layers together by sewing about ⅛″ from the outside edges of the embellished front piece.

5. Trim the orange square evenly to about ¼″ beyond the embellished front to create the Peek-a-Boo edging. Insert the pillow form and enjoy!

Tic-Tac-Toe Purse,
8$\frac{1}{2}$″ × 8$\frac{1}{2}$″,
Mary Stori, 2006

Back of purse

Tic-Tac-Toe Purse

Peek-a-Boo Edge

THESE SMALL GRAB-AND-GO PURSES ARE SO
EASY TO MAKE, YOU'LL WANT TO MAKE SEVERAL
SO YOU CAN HAVE THEM IN YOUR FAVORITE
COLOR COMBINATIONS. THEY ARE PERFECT AS
GIFTS FOR ALL AGES.

Materials

Refer to pages 5–9 for basic supplies.

- 1 rectangle 9″ × 13″ of red felted wool for front flap/purse back
- 1 rectangle 9″ × 16″ of red felted wool for lower front
- 1 rectangle 11″ × 14″ of chartreuse felted wool for lining/edging
- 1 strip 1″ × 36″ of red felted wool for strap (adjust length as necessary)
- 1 rectangle 14″ × 4″ of turquoise felted wool for appliqué

- 1 rectangle 9″ × 13″ of lightweight tear-away stabilizer for front flap/purse back
- 1 rectangle 9″ × 8″ of lightweight tear-away stabilizer for lower front
- ⅛ yard of paper-backed fusible web
- Size #11 yellow seed beads
- Nymo beading thread

Instructions

Refer to pages 10–18 for basic techniques.

PREPARATION

1. Use the method of your choice (pages 10–11) to make templates for the curved edges, using the patterns on Side A of the pullout at the back of the book.

2. Mark a rectangle 8″ × 12″ on the large piece of stabilizer. Mark a line 7½″ in from the line at one narrow end for the fold line. Use the templates to mark the front flap and bottom curves. Thread-baste the stabilizer to the 9″ × 13″ red piece, following the marked lines.

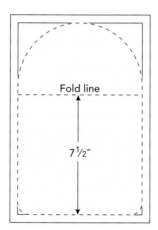

Mark stabilizer for front flap/purse back and baste to wool.

3. Mark ½″ in from 3 sides on the 9″ × 8″ piece of stabilizer to make a rectangle 8″ × 7½″ for the lower front. Use the bottom curve template to mark the bottom curves. Thread-baste the stabilizer to one end of the 9″ × 16″ red piece, following the marked lines.

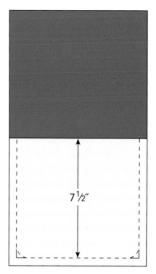

Mark stabilizer for lower front and baste to wool.

COLLAGE AND EMBELLISH

1. Use the Paper-Backed Fusible Web Method (page 12) to prepare the turquoise piece. Freehand cut 12 wavy strips, about ¼″ wide, varying the lengths from about 1½″ to 4″. Remove the paper, and arrange the strips in a tic-tac-toe design on the right side of the stabilized pieces.

2. Place a motif on each of the front flap, back, and lower front pieces. Fuse in place using a warm iron.

3. Embellish the wool strips and surrounding area as desired with yellow seed beads, using the Single Bead Backstitch (page 15).

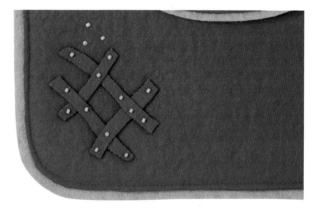

Embellish strips with beads.

4. Cut out the main body of the purse (front flap/back), following the outside basting line. **Do not cut the line at the fold—it is for reference.** Trim away about ¼″ of stabilizer from the outside edges.

PEEK-A-BOO EDGE

1. Center the trimmed front flap/back piece onto the chartreuse edging piece, securing with straight pins. Machine topstitch the layers together about ⅛″ from the outside edge. Remove the basting from the fold line.

Center and sew layers together.

2. Fold the piece for the lower front in half wrong sides together. Press to create a nice folded edge, and temporarily secure the layers with a few pins. Carefully cut out, following the basting lines. Trim away about ¼″ of the stabilizer from the outside edges. Topstitch the folded edge, if desired.

3. Make the strap by folding the long red strip lengthwise, with edges meeting in the middle. Press with a steam iron, and use straight pins to temporarily hold in place. Sew 2 lines of stitching lengthwise to secure the layers. Adjust the length as necessary.

4. To assemble the purse, turn the chartreuse piece wrong side up, and place the lower front piece on it, using the top-stitching as a guide. Pin the strap ends between the layers at each side, just below the fold. Machine topstitch the layers together about ⅛″ from the outside edge.

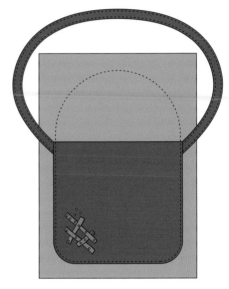

Assembly layout

5. Once all the stitching is completed, carefully trim the chartreuse piece to within a scant ¼″ of the purse to create the Peek-a-Boo edging.

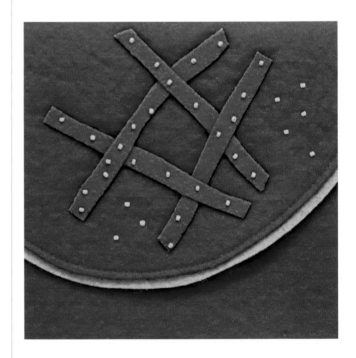

Star Bright,
14″ × 14″, Mary Stori, 2006

Star Bright

Wavy Cut Edge

GRAB YOUR BUTTON JAR AND BEADS TO MAKE THIS SIMPLE STAR WALLHANGING. THIS IS A WONDERFUL DESIGN FOR A PURSE OR PILLOW, TOO.

Materials

Refer to pages 5–9 for basic supplies.

- 1 square 13″ × 13″ of blue/black check wool felt for front
- 1 square 15″ × 15″ of gold wool felt for back/edging
- 1 square 13″ × 13″ of lightweight tear-away stabilizer
- ½ yard of paper-backed fusible web
- White buttons (approximately 135)
- Size #11 white seed beads
- Embroidery floss in gold
- Nymo beading thread
- Rotary cutter with decorative blade

Instructions

Refer to pages 10–18 for basic techniques.

PREPARATION

Mark a square 12″ × 12″ centered on the stabilizer. Trace the button placement pattern onto the stabilizer, using the pattern on Side B of the pullout at the back of the book. Center the star outline within the marked square. Use the Stabilizer Technique (page 11) to thread-baste the stabilizer to the blue/black front piece, following the marked lines.

COLLAGE AND EMBELLISH

Arrange and stitch the buttons to outline the shape of the star on the stabilized front piece. Continue adding buttons to outline the shape, and then fill in the center. When satisfied with their placement, embellish them with white seed beads, as described on page 16.

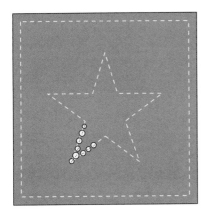

Audition button placement along star outline before securing with bead embellishing.

WAVY CUT EDGE

1. Remove as much of the stabilizer as possible from the embellished front piece. Cut a square 13″ × 13″ of paper-backed fusible web. Use a warm iron to fuse it to the wrong side of the front piece.

2. Cut the embellished front piece to measure 12″ × 12″, keeping the button star centered.

3. Center the front on the back piece. (*Note:* The back is cut larger than needed to allow for distortion and for the "oops" factor when trimming with a decorative rotary cutting blade.) Cover with a pressing cloth, and press with a hot iron around the outside of the star, just enough to hold the layers together. Let it cool. Turn over the piece, and complete the fusing process from the back.

4. Finish the outside edges of the front piece with hand blanket-stitching (page 13), using gold floss.

5. Use a rotary cutter fitted with a decorative blade to trim the back to measure 1″ beyond the embellished front on all sides.

6. Carefully (to avoid distortion of the unstabilized edge) attach 8 small buttons evenly spaced on each vertical side. Embellish with beads.

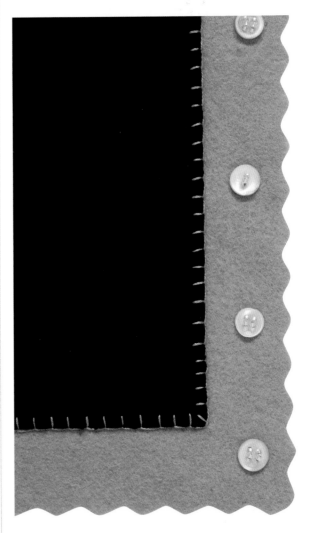

Finish edges with hand blanket-stitching; outer edges feature Wavy Cut Edge and bead-embellished buttons.

Lily Basket,
17″ × 17″,
Mary Stori, 2004

Lily Basket

Scallop Edge

ANTIQUE BUTTONS CREATE THE VINTAGE
BASKET FILLED WITH WARM YELLOW FLOWERS.
HAND BLANKET-STITCHING COMPLETES THE
VINTAGE LOOK.

Materials

Refer to pages 5–9 for basic supplies.

- 1 square 16″ × 16″ of red felted wool for front

- 1 square 18″ × 18″ of black felted wool for back/scallops

- 1 square 9″ × 9″ of green felted wool for stems

- Scraps of black and yellow felted wool for flowers

- 1 square 16″ × 16″ of lightweight tear-away stabilizer

- ⅓ yard of paper-backed fusible web

- White buttons (approximately 80)   ■ Size #11 white seed beads

- Embroidery thread or floss in black and red

- Nymo beading thread

- Freezer paper

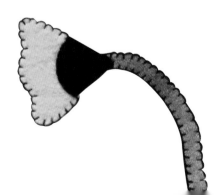

Instructions

Refer to pages 10–18 for basic techniques.

PREPARATION

Mark a square 15″ × 15″ centered on the stabilizer. Trace the button placement pattern onto the stabilizer, using the pattern on Side B of the pullout at the back of the book. Center the basket outline about 1″ above the marked square. (The handle will be added later.) Use the Stabilizer Technique (page 11) to baste the stabilizer to the red front piece, following the marked lines.

COLLAGE AND EMBELLISH

1. Use the Paper-Backed Fusible Web Method (page 12) to prepare the stem and flower motifs, using the patterns from Side B of the pullout. (*Note:* The stems are cut freehand.) Remove the paper backing, and arrange the flowers and stems, making sure that the top row of the buttons will hide the lower ends of the stems (refer to the project photo).

2. Fuse the motifs onto the stabilized front piece using a warm iron. Finish the edges with hand or machine blanket-stitching (page 13), using black thread.

3. Arrange and stitch the buttons to fill the shape of the flowerpot. Create the handle by arranging the buttons in a large arch that spans from each side of the top row of buttons. The size and number of buttons available will help determine the shape of the handle. To add interest, overlap a stem with a few buttons. When satisfied with the placement, stitch and embellish the buttons with white beads, as described on page 16.

SCALLOP EDGE

To position a scallop at each corner, the completed center should measure an uneven number, for example, 15″ × 15″.

1. Cut the embellished front piece to measure 15″ × 15″. Trim the stabilizer about 1″ away from the outside edges.

2. Prepare a freezer-paper template (page 11) from the pattern on the pullout for the scallop edging. Cut out the shape, adding an extra ¼″ around the outside. However, to gain a better understanding of the process that I use to create scallops, consider working through the steps of Planning Your Own Scallop Edge (next page) so you can make your own on future projects.

3. When you are satisfied with the appearance of the scallops, press the template to the backing fabric. Cut through the freezer-paper template, following the curved lines of the scallops. The space between each scallop allows just enough room to pivot the scissors. Remove the paper.

4. Center the embellished front on the scallop back. Temporarily secure these layers using your favorite method, such as hand basting or adhesive basting spray. Permanently join the layers by sewing along the outside edge of the embellished front with hand or machine blanket-stitching, using black thread. Decorate and stabilize the scallops by blanket-stitching with red thread.

Secure front to back with hand blanket-stitch; scallop edges finish piece.

Planning Your Own Scallop Edge

1. Mark a square 15″ × 15″ onto freezer paper. Mark 3 more squares, each $\frac{1}{2}$″ outside the previous marked square. Mark a diagonal line at each corner, from the outside of the 15″ × 15″ square to the outside edge of the 17″ × 17″ square. Cut on the outside lines to make a square template 18″ × 18″.

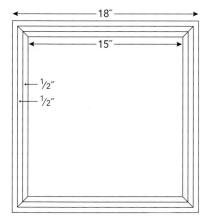

Mark freezer-paper template with reference lines.

2. Fold the template twice to crease horizontally and vertically. The scallop in the middle of each border will be centered on a fold line. On the 16″ × 16″ square, make reference dots $1\frac{1}{8}$″ on either side of the center fold. Working outward from the reference dot, measure and mark this sequence: $\frac{1}{8}$″, $2\frac{1}{4}$″, $\frac{1}{8}$″, $2\frac{1}{4}$″, $\frac{1}{8}$″.

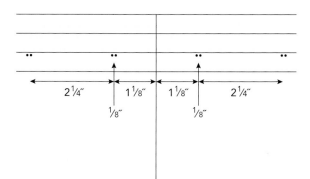

Mark reference dots for scallop placement.

3. Use a compass, a circle template, or the edge of a bowl to draw scallops that fit within each of the $2\frac{1}{4}$″ divisions along all of the sides. Round off the top of each scallop along the line of the 17″ × 17″ square, and continue drawing the curve down to meet the 16″ × 16″ square. Repeat using a larger circle to create the scallop at each corner. Work with pencil and eraser, aiming for uniform sizes. It's easier to develop $\frac{1}{8}$th of the pattern and use that to trace the remaining sections.

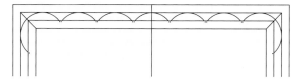

Mark scallops between reference dots.

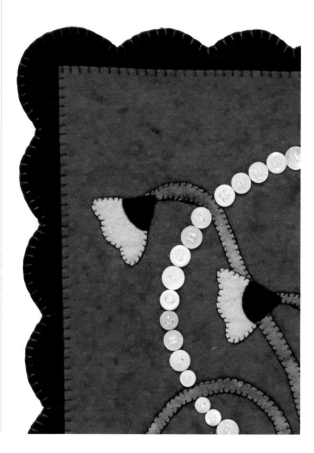

Half Moon Dreams,
14˝ diameter,
Mary Stori, 2005

Half Moon Dreams

Circular One-Piece Tongue Edge

WHAT CHILD WOULDN'T LOVE THIS DARLING WALL
QUILT TO FALL ASLEEP UNDER AFTER HEARING HIS
OR HER FAVORITE BEDTIME STORY?

Materials

Refer to pages 5–9 for basic supplies.

- 1 square 13˝ × 13˝ of red felted wool for front

- 1 square 15˝ × 15˝ of purple felted wool for back/edging

- 1 square 5˝ × 5˝ of yellow felted wool for bear body and leg

- 2 rectangles 3˝ × 5˝ of yellow felted wool for head and arm

- Scrap of purple felted wool for stars

- 1 square 13˝ × 13˝ of lightweight tear-away stabilizer

- ¼ yard of paper-backed fusible web

- White buttons (approximately 125)

- 1 small black button

- Size #11 seed beads in white, black, and purple

- 2 size #6 black seed beads

- AURIfil Lana thread in black and red

- Nymo beading thread

- Freezer paper

Instructions

Refer to pages 10–18 for basic techniques.

PREPARATION

Mark a circle 12˝ in diameter centered onto the stabilizer. Trace the button placement pattern onto the stabilizer, using the pattern on Side B of the pullout at the back of the book. Use the Stabilizer Technique (page 11) to thread-baste the stabilizer to the red front piece, following the marked lines.

COLLAGE AND EMBELLISH

1. Arrange and stitch the buttons to fill the shape of the moon on the stabilized front piece. The sizes of your buttons may require some adjustments to this shape; lightly redraw lines as necessary as the buttons are auditioned for placement. (*Note:* Be sure to keep the moon within the marked circle, using the project photo as your placement guide.) The basting is your cutting line for the center circle, so don't get too close. When satisfied with the placement, embellish the buttons with white beads, as described on page 16.

2. Use the Paper-Backed Fusible Web Method (page 12) to prepare the teddy bear's body and leg, using the patterns on the pullout. The patterns have been reversed for fusible web appliqué.

3. Use the Freezer-Paper Method (page 12) and the patterns on the pullout to prepare templates for the head and arm. Cut a rectangle 3˝ × 5˝ of fusible web, and fuse the 2 yellow rectangles together. Press the freezer-paper templates to the fused yellow rectangles, and cut out on the marked lines. Hand blanket-stitch (page 13) the arm edges, using black thread.

4. Arrange the prepared teddy bear motifs onto the moon by referring to the project photo. Set aside the head and arm, and use a warm iron to fuse the body and leg onto the front. Hand blanket-stitch along the edges of the motifs, using black thread.

5. Reposition the head onto the teddy bear's body, securing with a straight pin. Attach the lower portion of the head to the front by hand blanket-stitching from A to B (refer to the head pattern), and then continue stitching, catching only the edges of the yellow wool. The top portion of the head will remain free. Use the Washer/Nut Technique (page 16) to attach the beads for the eye. Attach a bead for the nose.

6. Attach the arm to the bear's body, using the black button and black seed beads.

7. Use the Paper-Backed Fusible Web Method to prepare the purple stars, using the patterns on Side B of the pullout. Arrange as desired on the embellished front within the basted circle, fuse and embellish using the Single Bead Backstitch (page 15).

CIRCULAR ONE-PIECE TONGUE EDGE

1. Cut the embellished front piece by following the marked circle lines on the stabilizer. Trim the stabilizer from the edges.

2. Create a template for the scallop edging by drawing a 12″ circle onto the dull side of a piece of freezer paper. Next, draw another circle to extend 1″ beyond the first, making a 14″ circle. Draw a third circle ½″ beyond the second to make a 15″ circle. Cut out the template by following the lines of the last circle.

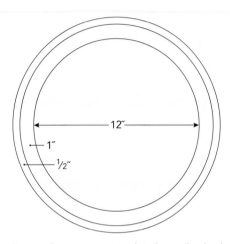

Prepare freezer-paper template for scallop back.

3. Fold the paper into 16 evenly divided sections. Use a compass, a circle template, or the edge of a bowl to draw a scallop to fit within the 1″ space (between the first and second circle), or use the single scallop pattern on the Side B of the pullout. Draw a scallop in each of the sections.

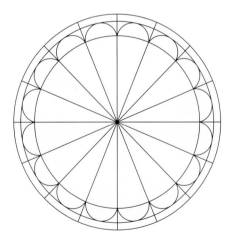

Fold template to divide evenly into 16 sections, and trace scallops in each.

4. Press the freezer-paper template to the purple back piece. Cut through the freezer-paper template, following the curved lines of the scallops. Remove the paper.

5. Center and baste the embellished front to the back using your favorite method. If spray adhesive is your choice, be sure to only spray the wrong side of the center section. Permanently secure the outer edge to the back with purple seed beads spaced about ½″ apart using the Single Bead Backstitch. Decorate and stabilize the scallop edges by hand blanket-stitching with red thread.

Seed beads secure center to back; hand blanket-stitching finishes scallop edges.

A Tisket, a Tasket,
14½″ × 14½″,
Mary Stori, 2004

A Tisket, a Tasket

Double Scallop Edge

THE SCALLOP SHAPE OF THIS PIECE IS DRAMATI-
CALLY OUTLINED, SHOWING OFF THE GENTLE
CURVES. THE BUTTON FLOWERS TOP GRACEFULLY
CURVING STEMS THAT ARE INTERTWINED WITH
THE BASKET HANDLE.

Materials

Refer to pages 5–9 for basic supplies.

- 1 square 15″ × 15″ of green felted wool for front
- 1 square 16″ × 16″ of dark green felted wool for back/edging
- 1 square 9″ × 9″ of brown felted wool for stems
- 1 square 7″ × 7″ of light brown felted wool for basket
- 1 square 15″ × 15″ of lightweight tear-away stabilizer
- 1 yard of paper-backed fusible web
- White buttons (approximately 80)
- Size #11 matte white and opaque black seed beads
- 12 size #6 matte white seed beads
- Embroidery thread or floss in black and 3 tones of brown
- Nymo beading thread

Instructions

Refer to pages 10–18 for basic techniques.

PREPARATION

The final edging shape is incorporated into the design at its beginning, rather than creating a scallop template after the embellished front piece is completed. You can create any scallop shape by folding a paper template into equal or unequal divisions and rounding off the outside edges with a circle template or circular object. A pattern is provided for this project.

Trace the scallop onto the stabilizer, using the pattern from Side B of the pullout at the back of the book. Thread-baste the stabilizer to the green front piece, following the marked lines.

COLLAGE AND EMBELLISH

1. Use the Paper-Backed Fusible Web Method (page 12) to prepare the stems and basket motif, using the pattern on Side B of the pullout. (*Note:* The stems are cut freehand.) Arrange the motifs on the stabilized front piece, referring to the project photo as your guide. Notice some of the stems are positioned over the handle of the basket, while some are placed under it.

2. When you are satisfied with the placement, fuse using a warm iron. Finish the edges with hand or machine blanket-stitching (page 13).

3. Arrange and stitch small white buttons to create flower heads at the ends of each stem. Embellish with white seed beads, as instructed on page 16.

4. Add a line of black seed beads along the front of the basket, and stitch a few to add texture to the handle.

5. Use 3 strands of brown embroidery floss in light, dark, and medium and the Stem Stitch (page 14) to add a few tendrils growing from the stems.

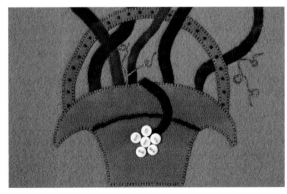

Embroidery and beads add texture and interest.

DOUBLE SCALLOP EDGE

1. To get a good bond when adding the backing, trim away as much of the stabilizer as possible.

2. Cut a square 15″ × 15″ of paper-backed fusible web. Trace the scallop pattern onto the paper side. Cut out the shape, adding an extra ¼″. Place the embellished front face down on a terrycloth towel on the pressing surface. Center the piece of fusible web on it, paper side up, and press. Let it cool before handling. Cut through the fusible web template, following the curved lines of the scallops. Remove the paper.

3. Center the embellished front face up on the back piece. Cover with a pressing cloth, and press the edges with a hot iron, just enough to hold the layers together. Let cool. Turn over the piece, and complete the fusing process from the wrong side.

4. Secure the edge of the front to the back with beads, keeping the stitches on the back of the project as invisible as possible. Sew white seed beads, using the Single Bead Backstitch (page 15), about ¼″ apart along the edge. At each inside curve, add a large and small seed bead unit using the Washer/Nut technique (page 16).

5. Working from the right side, use sharp scissors to carefully, and as accurately as possible, trim the back to within ⅛″–¼″ of the front piece.

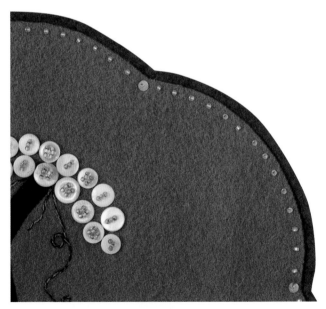

Trim darker green back to create frame

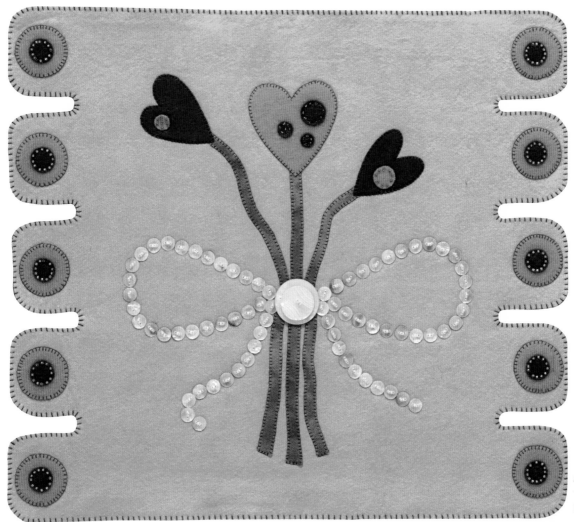

Buttons & Bow,
18″ × 16″,
Mary Stori, 2004

Buttons & Bow

Built-In Tongues Edge

THE BUILT-IN TONGUE EDGING PROVIDES THE CHARMING LOOK OF A TRADITIONAL PENNY RUG. THE BUTTON BOW ADDS A SOFT LUSTER TO THIS NOSTALGIC PIECE.

Materials

Refer to pages 5–9 for basic supplies.

- 2 rectangles 19″ × 17″ of gold felted wool for front and back
- 1 rectangle 12″ × 5″ of green felted wool for stems
- 1 square 8″ × 8″ of orange felted wool for flower and circles
- 1 square 7″ × 7″ of blue felted wool for flowers and circles
- 1 rectangle 19″ × 17″ of lightweight tear-away stabilizer
- ⅓ yard of paper-backed fusible web
- 1 white button about 1½″ in diameter
- 1 white button about 1″ in diameter
- White buttons ½″ in diameter (approximately 75)
- Size #11 seed beads in white, orange, and blue
- Embroidery thread or floss in black
- Nymo beading thread

Instructions

Refer to pages 10–18 for basic techniques.

PREPARATION

1. Mark a rectangle 18″ × 16″ centered on the stabilizer. Draw a reference line on each short side, 2¼″ inside the marked rectangle. Thread-baste the stabilizer to a gold piece for the front, following all the marked lines.

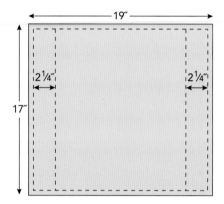

Baste stabilizer to front, following marked lines.

2. Working on the right side of the wool, use a removable marking tool, such as chalk, to lightly mark horizontal and vertical center reference lines.

COLLAGE AND EMBELLISH

1. Use the Paper-Backed Fusible Web Method (page 12) to prepare the stems and flower motifs, using the patterns on Side B of the pullout at the back of the book. The patterns have been reversed for fusible web appliqué. (*Note:* The stems are cut freehand.) Place the center stem along the marked vertical line, with the lower end of the stem about 1½″ from the basted line. Position the 2 remaining stems on each side of the center stem. Arrange the flower heads by referring to the project photo.

2. Fuse the motifs onto the stabilized front piece using a warm iron. Finish the edges with hand or machine blanket-stitching, using black thread (page 13).

3. Embellish the edges of the orange and blue circles with contrasting colors of seed beads, stitched about ⅛″ apart using the Single Bead Backstitch (page 15).

Heart-shaped flower heads feature machine blanket-stitching and beading.

4. Use the Marking-Tool Technique (page 11) to transfer the button placement pattern onto the wool. Leaving room for the large buttons in the center, trace the bow motif, then repeat by drawing another one reversed. Vary the ends, if desired.

5. Stack the 2 large buttons (largest at the bottom) over the stem in the center of the marked shape of the bow. Attach by following the directions on page 16. Arrange and stitch the smaller buttons along the marked shape of the bow, and embellish with beads when you are satisfied with their placement.

BUILT-IN TONGUES EDGE

1. Use the method of your choice (pages 10–12) to prepare the template for the tongues, using the pattern on the pullout. Be sure to mark the location of the center.

2. Trace 5 tongues along each short side of the embellished front. To keep the placement as uniform as possible, position the center tongue first. Place it within the 2¼″ basted lines, matching the center of the template to the marked horizontal line. Trace the template using chalk. Next, position the template to mark the tongues at the ends. Mark the last 2 tongues. The space between each of the tongues is approximately ¼″ wide. **Mark the units, but do not cut them out.**

Position and trace tongue template evenly along each side.

3. Use the Paper-Backed Fusible Web Method to prepare the orange and blue circles, using the patterns on Side B of the pullout. Center the circles on each of the marked tongues, and fuse. Finish the edges of the orange circles with blanket-stitching, and use orange seed beads to embellish the edges of the blue circles.

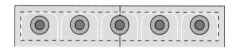

To prevent distortion, appliqué and embellish the tongues before cutting shapes.

4. Trim away as much of the stabilizer as possible. Baste the gold back piece to the wrong side of the embellished front piece, matching the raw edges.

Fusible web is not recommended for putting together the layers because the heat might cause the marked lines to disappear or, even worse, become permanent. Therefore, the easiest way to secure these layers together is by spray basting or ample thread-basting by hand.

5. Use small, sharp scissors to carefully cut out the tongues by following the marked lines and rounding the corners. Use a rotary cutting tool to trim the top and bottom edges, straight and even, following the basted lines.

6. Secure the layers together along the edges with hand blanket-stitching.

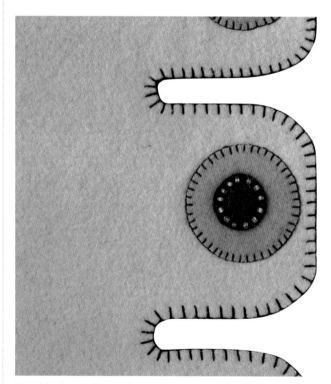

Keep blanket stitches uniform in size and fairly close together.

Hearts & Flowers,
19″ × 19″,
Mary Stori, 2005

Hearts & Flowers

Individual Tongues Edge

THIS LOVELY WALLHANGING FEATURES A BUTTON HEART SURROUNDING LONG-STEMMED POSIES. THE PENNY RUG-STYLE EDGING ADDS TO THE RUSTIC CHARM.

Materials

Refer to pages 5–9 for basic supplies.

- 1 square 15½″ × 15½″ of black felted wool for front

- 1 square 14½″ × 14½″ of black felted wool for back

- 4 strips 21″ × 2¾″ of black felted wool for tongues

- 1 rectangle 5″ × 8″ of green felted wool for stems

- 1 square 10″ × 10″ of blue felted wool for circles and flowers

- Scraps of purple felted wool for flower centers

- 1 square 15½″ × 15½″ of lightweight tear-away stabilizer
- ¾ yard of paper-backed fusible web
- White buttons (approximately 85)
- Size #11 seed beads in white and blue
- AURIfil Lana thread in black and blue
- Nymo beading thread
- Freezer paper

Instructions

Refer to pages 10–18 for basic techniques.

PREPARATION

Mark a square 14½″ × 14½″ centered on the stabilizer. Trace the button placement pattern onto the stabilizer, using the pattern from Side B of the pullout at the back of the book. Center the heart outline within the marked square. Thread-baste the stabilizer to the black front piece, following all the marked lines.

COLLAGE AND EMBELLISH

1. Use the Paper-Backed Fusible Web Method (page 12) to prepare the stems. (*Note:* The stems are cut freehand.) Arrange the motifs on the stabilized front piece within the basted lines, referring to the project photo as your guide.

2. Fuse the stems in place using a warm iron. Finish the edges with hand or machine blanket-stitching (page 13).

3. Use the Freezer Paper Method (page 12) to prepare the flower motifs, using the patterns on Side B of the pullout.

4. Center and stack a purple center onto a blue flower head, and arrange this on the stems, as shown in the project photo or as desired. Attach using the Bead Cluster technique (page 17).

5. Arrange and stitch the buttons, centered along the basted heart outline. When satisfied with the placement, embellish the buttons with white beads, as described on page 16.

INDIVIDUAL TONGUES EDGE

1. Cut the embellished front piece to measure 14½″ × 14½″. Trim the stabilizer about ¼″ from each edge.

2. Thread-baste the embellished front to the black back piece.

> **tip**
>
> *Don't adhere the front and back layers together with any kind of adhesive. You'll need to slip the end of each of the tongues between the layers to complete the edging treatment.*

3. Use the method of your choice (pages 10–12) to make a template for the tongues, using the pattern on Side B of the pullout. Use a removable marking tool to trace 8 tongues each onto 2 of the long black strips. Allow a ¼″ seam allowance at the flat end of the tongues, and leave a scant ¼″ between them. (*Note:* The strip is cut larger than necessary to allow for the spacing and the seam allowance and to make the curve easier to trace on the felted wool.)

Trace tongue template on wool strip.

4. Use the Paper-Backed Fusible Web Method to prepare 16 blue circles, using the pattern on Side B of the pullout. Position a circle on each of the marked tongues, and fuse using a warm iron. Finish the edges of the circles with hand or machine blanket-stitching. Center a button on each circle, and embellish it with white beads.

Position circles on tongues; embellish with embroidery and beaded buttons.

Note: Before proceeding with the following step, test to be sure your markings will not disappear or discolor. If you have a problem, use spray adhesive instead of fusible web to attach the layers.

5. Cut 2 pieces 21″ × 2¾″ of paper-backed fusible web. Fuse one piece to each of the remaining black strips. Let cool, and remove the paper. Place the embellished black pieces face down on a terrycloth towel on the pressing surface. Matching the raw edges, place the prepared black pieces on top, with the web side down. Fuse the strips together.

6. Cut out the tongues along the marked lines, allowing a ¼″ seam allowance on the flat end. Use the Blanket Stitch to sew the curved edges, using either black or blue thread and beginning and ending at the top of each side.

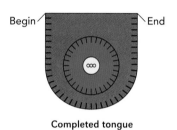

Completed tongue

7. Slip the seam allowance of the tongues between the layers of the front and back pieces, lining up the sides evenly with the edge of the corner. Pin or thread-baste to temporarily hold them in place.

8. Position and baste the remaining tongues, referring to the project photo as your placement guide. Attach the edges of the front and back together with hand blanket-stitching, using blue thread.

Secure layers and tongues with hand blanket-stitching.

tip

Blanket-stitch along the edges of the front and back layers as usual, but when you reach the tongues, stitch the front edge, catching only the top edge of the tongues. Stitch in this manner around the entire piece. To finish the edges on the back, blanket-stitch the unstitched areas.

Resources

**Books, DVDs, and Videos
by Mary Stori**
www.marystori.com

WoolFelt
National Nonwovens
www.woolfelt.com

Wool Fabric
Moda Fabrics
www.modafabrics.com

Needles & Scissors
Jean S. Lyle
www.jslyle.com

Circle Templates
Karen Kay Buckley's Perfect Circles
www.karenkaybuckley.com

AURIfil and Embroidery Threads
That Thread Shop
www.thatthreadshop.com

Beads and Shell Buttons
Fire Mountain Gems
www.firemountaingems.com

Embroidery Frames
Q-Snap Corporation
www.qsnap.com

About the Author

Mary Stori is an internationally recognized quiltmaker, fashion designer, instructor, lecturer, and quilt show judge who has authored a cookbook and six quilting books. Her most recent releases are a DVD, *Mary Stori Teaches You Beading on Fabric* (2006), *All-in-One Beading Buddy* (2005), and *Beading Basics* (2004). She was awarded 2004 Teacher of the Year by The Professional Quilter.

Mary has written extensively, and her work has appeared in scores of quilt magazines and publications. Her award-winning work has been widely exhibited both nationally and internationally. She has appeared on HGTV's *Simply Quilts* and *Sew Perfect*. An entire episode of *Fon's & Porter's Love of Quilting* featured her beaded quilts. She designed the Mary Stori Collection for Kona Bay Fabrics, as well as her own line of stencils for Quilting Creations.

Traveling worldwide to present lectures and workshops keeps her motivated. Visit Mary at www.marystori.com.

Also by Mary Stori

Note: Fabrics used in the quilts shown may not be currently available as fabric manufacturers keep most fabrics in print for only a short time.

**For a list of other fine books from
C&T Publishing, ask for a free catalog:**
C&T Publishing, Inc.
P.O. Box 1456, Lafayette, CA 94549
(800) 284-1114
Email: ctinfo@ctpub.com
Website: www.ctpub.com

C&T
MEDIA SERVICES

C&T Publishing's professional photography services are now available to the public. Visit us at www.ctmediaservices.com.

For quilting supplies:
Cotton Patch
1025 Brown Ave., Lafayette, CA 94549
(800) 835-4418 or (925) 283-7883
Email: CottonPa@aol.com
Website: www.quiltusa.com

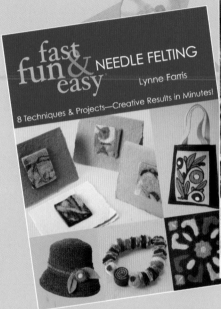

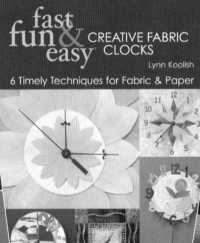
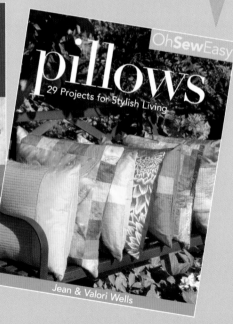